A SHORT HISTORY OF

Ireland's Rebels

EIGHTEEN MEN AND WOMEN WHO LIVED

AND DIED FOR IRELAND.

These are the stirring stories of outstanding men and women who defied an unsympathetic establishment in their struggle for self-determination. Through the centuries these rebels – Protestant and Catholic, rich and poor – endured imprisonment, were exiled to Australia or the USA, or gave their lives, all for the cause of freedom.

Morgan Llywelyn is the acclaimed author of many historical novels for adults, including *Lion of Ireland*, *Druids*, *On Raven's Wing* and *1916*, a novel based on the Easter Rising. Her award-winning books for children include *Brian Boru*, *Strongbow* and *The Young Rebels*. Morgan lives in Dublin.

A SHORT HISTORY OF
Ireland's Rebels

MORGAN LLYWELYN

THE O'BRIEN PRESS
DUBLIN

First published in smaller format as *A Pocket History of Irish Rebels* in 2000 by
The O'Brien Press Ltd,
12 Terenure Road East, Rathgar, Dublin 6
Tel: +353 1 4923333; Fax: +353 1 4922777
E-mail: books@obrien.ie
Website: www.obrien.ie
Reprinted 2001, 2003, 2006.
This edition first published 2013 by The O'Brien Press Ltd

ISBN: 978-1-84717-370-6

British Library Cataloguing-in-Publication Data
A catalogue record for this title is available from The British Library

5 6 7 8 9 10
13 14 15 16

Editing, typesetting, layout and design: The O'Brien Press Ltd
Printed and bound by CPI Group (UK) Ltd, Croydon, CR0 4YY
The paper in this book is produced using pulp from managed forests

Picture credits
The author and publisher wish to thank the following for permission to reproduce visual materials. **Front cover:** 1798 memorial statue, *Fuascailt*, courtesy of Getty Images. **Picture section:** The National Library of Ireland, p.1 (both), p.2 (both), p.3 (both), p.4 (both), p.5 (top and bottom), p.6 (bottom), p.7 (top and bottom); The National Museum of Ireland, p.6 (top); Cork Public Museum, p.7 (middle); Pacemaker Press International, p.8 (top); *The Irish Times*, p.8 (bottom).

CONTENTS

INTRODUCTION

From the dawn of history there has been a strong streak of the rebel in the Celtic character. The Oxford English Dictionary defines a rebel as a 'person who fights against, resists, or refuses allegiance to, the established government; person or thing that resists authority or control.'

Early Celtic art provides a visual demonstration of this tendency. Scorning right angles and straight lines, those classic symbols of control, the La Tène sculptors and craftsmen of the Celtic Bronze Age used flowing curvilinear shapes to give a feeling of unfettered freedom. Celtic art swoops and spirals, it cannot be contained.

Julius Caesar encountered the Celtic proclivity for resisting authority when he set out to conquer Gaul. The great Celtic warlord Vercingetorix fought the imposition of Roman 'order' with every fibre of his being. The two viewpoints were irreconcilable. Hundreds of thousands of Celts were ruthlessly exterminated as Caesar enforced his will.

In time the freedom-loving Celts were forced to the western fringe of Europe, making their last stand along the Atlantic seaboard. The histories of Scotland, Wales and particularly Ireland ring with heroic tales, both ancient and modern, of men and women who refused to submit to foreign dominance. Taken individually, most of these stories are tragic. Observed as a whole, they say something magnificent about the human spirit.

The 18 rebels discussed in *A Pocket History of Irish Rebels* span the centuries from the sixteenth to the twentieth. Theirs is the story of Ireland's long struggle against English domination, the most enduring of all Celtic rebellions. At the beginning of the 21st century, 26 of Ireland's counties comprise a sovereign and free republic.

CHAPTER 1

Thomas FitzGerald,
Lord Offaly and 10th Earl of Kildare
(1513–1537)

'Silken Thomas'

When the Normans invaded Ireland in the twelfth century they were entering a land well accustomed to rebellion. Kingship in Ireland was not hereditary, but elective, a king being selected from among the eligible members of the ruling clan. This ancient Celtic form of quasi-democracy did not guarantee stability, however. Irish provincial kings occasionally rebelled against their Ard Rí, or High King; tribal kings even more frequently rebelled against the kings of the provinces.

The argument between Dermot MacMurrough, king of the province of Leinster, and his Ard Rí, Ruadhri Ó Connor, was the causative factor for the Norman invasion. When the Ard Rí stripped Dermot of his kingdom, MacMurrough invited Norman mercenaries, led by Richard de Clare, 'Strongbow', to come to Ireland to win it back for him. As a result the Normans acquired vast tracts of land and all the power that went with it; power that would in time lead them to rebel against their own overlord, the King of England.

The FitzGeralds of Ireland were descended from Maurice Fitz

Gerald – Fitz meaning 'son of' – who had accompanied Strongbow to Ireland. The family, collectively known as the Geraldines, split into two main branches. Senior members of the Leinster branch assumed the title of Earl of Kildare, and the Munster branch, Earl of Desmond.

The Geraldines intermarried with the native Irish as well as English nobility. Garrett FitzGerald, 8th Earl of Kildare (1477–1513), was an outstanding example of mixed Anglo-Irish stock, combining the best qualities of both races. He earned the sobriquet of 'the Great Earl' and wielded great influence quite independent of the English Crown. He also made powerful enemies. Accused of setting fire to the cathedral at Cashel in County Tipperary, the Great Earl replied, 'By my troth, I would never have done it but I thought the Bishop was in it.'

The King of England, upon being assured that all Ireland could not govern this man, replied, 'Then let this man govern all Ireland,' and appointed him Lord Deputy. FitzGerald remained Lord Deputy, with some interruptions, under Edward IV, Richard III, Henry VII – who nicknamed him 'my rebel' – and Henry VIII. These were turbulent times for any man to survive, yet he did.

After the Great Earl's death Henry VIII appointed Garrett's son Gerald to serve as Lord Deputy, feeling this was the best way to control the Kildare Geraldines. But the Geraldines would not be controlled. Eventually, Gerald was arrested for conspiring in a plot with his cousin, the Earl of Desmond, to drive the English out of Ireland. Before departing Dublin for imprisonment in the Tower of London, Gerald FitzGerald appointed his 20-year-old son Thomas to serve as Vice-Deputy.

Thomas was described by contemporaries as 'a man of great

natural beauty, tall and personable, with an amiable countenance, and of nature flexible and kind.' He also possessed a full measure of youthful recklessness.

Upon hearing rumours that his father was about to be 'made a head shorter' in the Tower, Thomas flung down the Sword of State in the Council Chamber and cried, 'I am none of Henry his deputy, I am his foe!' His councillors urged caution, and rightly. The rumours, it later transpired, were actually part of a plot by English intriguers who had been attempting to undermine the House of Kildare for generations.

But Thomas would not listen to advice. He assembled a company of 120 horsemen and outfitted them in grand style, including silken hangings on their helmets. With this cavalry and over 800 foot soldiers he paraded through Dublin. The nickname of 'Silken Thomas' dates from this occasion. With a less colourful nickname he might have become just one more rebel in Irish history.

At St Mary's Abbey, Thomas FitzGerald formally renounced allegiance to the King and declared war on the English government. The Mayor of Dublin was ordered to arrest him, but the city had been swept by plague and there were not enough men to carry out the order. Archbishop Alen, who had played a major part in the downfall of Gerald FitzGerald, tried to escape the city and the young man's wrath. In the attempt to capture him the Archbishop was killed instead, an event which resulted in the excommunication of Silken Thomas from the Church.

Although the insurrection was a serious one and lasted for almost three years, it was destined to failure from the first. The common people loved Thomas for his courage and physical beauty.

But the other great Anglo-Irish lords failed to support him. He managed to raise an army of some 7000 men and was promised help from both Spain and Scotland, but neither materialised. Thomas's excommunication weighed heavily against him.

Anticipating an English attack, Silken Thomas strengthened the fortifications of Maynooth Castle to an extent that might have proved impregnable to artillery. Instead it fell to betrayal, that of his foster-brother, who had been left in charge of the castle while Thomas went to gather more troops.

Ironically the betrayer himself was among those executed by the victorious English, who mounted the heads of the castle's defenders on spikes. They jokingly referred to this as 'the Pardon of Maynooth'. With the seizure of his castle, Silken Thomas's army melted away. Lord Leonard Grey forced him to surrender by burning him out of a small wooden fortress he had built for himself.

As Thomas was the step-nephew of Lord Grey, the young man hoped for favourable terms for the family. But in this he was disappointed. After Silken Thomas was sent to the Tower of London, Lord Grey accepted a bribe to seize his five uncles also. Two of them had opposed the rebellion from the first, but it made no difference. All five were hanged, drawn and quartered at Tyburn in 1537. Silken Thomas only survived them by five months, then met the same fate.

The destruction of the senior adult male members of the family had the intended effect. The Leinster Geraldines were effectively broken.

CHAPTER 2

Granuaile (c.1530–1603)

'The Pirate Queen'

Irish history is studded with remarkable women, from Brian Ború's wife Gormlaith to Constance Markievicz. The woman whom the English called Grace O'Malley was unique. A working pirate and a leader of men in a patriarchal culture, she was also the first of our great female rebels. Her justification for rebellion was neither political nor idealistic. It was a simple matter of survival.

Granuaile, to use her Irish name, was born into an ancient Gaelic society that would become extinct within her lifetime. The Brehon Law, which pre-dated Christianity in Ireland by many centuries, was still at least nominally in effect throughout much of the land. Brehon Law entitled women to parity with men in many respects, including the ownership of property. In earlier times they had also led their tribes and taken part in combat, although by the sixteenth century these exploits were dim memories.

The discovery of the New World was encouraging colonial ambitions and stimulating sea trade as never before. Under Henry VIII, England had undertaken shipbuilding at an unprecedented rate. For this they needed timber, and Ireland was almost entirely covered with primordial hardwood forests. The fact that those lands belonged to the individual Irish clans was immaterial to the Tudor monarchs. Ireland was a resource to be exploited.

On the west coast of Ireland in the province of Connacht, in what is now County Mayo, lived a powerful Irish clan who made their principle living from the sea. They were hereditary lords of a region called the Umhalls, which included the area around Clew Bay. The earliest mention of the clan is in 1123, when they were referred to in the Annals of the Four Masters as Uí Máille.

Granuaile's father was an Uí Máille chieftain known as Dubhdarra – the Black Oak. Under Brehon Law a chieftain did not automatically inherit his title, but was elected from amongst the contenders within the senior branch of his clan. Dubhdarra owned a fleet of galleys and caravels, as well as smaller, hide-covered curraghs. With these he engaged in fishing and foreign trade. He also sold licences to the English, Spanish and French fleets that wanted to fish in his territory.

When Granuaile was 16 she married Dónal O'Flaherty, head of another prominent seafaring clan. The marriage was not a happy one. Dónal had a truculent disposition which did not help his ambitions to become ruler of all Connacht. When he was implicated in the murder of an ally of Dubhdarra's, he lost the support of his wife's people. One needed to be both a spectacular warrior and an adept politician to rise to the kingship, and Dónal was neither. As the years passed he even proved to be inept at leading his own men.

Granuaile bore Dónal three children during their marriage and was mistress of his castles at Bunowen and Ballinahinch, but these responsibilities did not exhaust her great energy. Eventually she took over her husband's role as leader of his clan during the pirate raids for which they were justly feared. Galway city had closed its gates to the O'Flaherty clan, and so any foreign vessel attempting to use Galway port was considered fair game.

Although by the sixteenth century the life of a Gaelic woman was expected to be one of total domesticity, from the start Granuaile took to her new role. She captained her ships herself, sailing north to Scotland or south to Spain in all weathers. She also won the loyalty of as wild and rough a band of men as could be found anywhere. Her exploits of piracy and her skill in the political infighting so much a part of Gaelic life became legend.

Around 1570, when Dónal O'Flaherty was slain by members of the Joyce clan for having seized one of their castles, Granuaile successfully defended the island fortress, which became known as the Hen's Castle. But while the Irish were engaged in their unceasing tribal conflicts, a larger war was building over the horizon. Elizabeth Tudor was now Queen of England, and meant to complete the conquest of Ireland which her forebears had begun. Through a mixture of force, bribery and intimidation, the queen's administrators gradually usurped the power of the local chieftains.

English soldiers besieged Granuaile in the Hen's Castle. She escaped and returned to her father's territory. There she gathered a band of some 200 men, many of them followers of her late husband, and went into the trade-and-piracy business for herself. Operating out of an Uí Máille stronghold on Clew Bay, Granuaile monitored foreign shipping along Ireland's west coast and charged for safe passage through the waters she controlled, or offered a pilot service – for a price. From those who refused either offer she extracted plunder.

Meanwhile, in England, Elizabeth had no thought of Granuaile – she was busy benefiting from the successes of her own stable of pirates, which included Francis Drake.

With an eye to strengthening her power base Granuaile next married Richard Burke, known as Richard-in-Iron, whose clan held considerable territory north of Clew Bay. They had one son, Tibbot, or Theobald as he was later called, who was born around 1567, supposedly on board a ship during an encounter with Turkish pirates.

After marrying Richard, Granuaile spent most of her time on land in the Burke castle known as Rockfleet, on the north shore of Clew Bay. The castle is intact to this day, spare and stark and defiant, an evocative symbol of the woman who once lived there.

Granuaile eventually divorced Richard Burke as she was entitled to do under Brehon Law, but kept the highly defensible Rockfleet for herself. When Richard died she ruled his followers and her own from there, becoming in effect a she-king, or *bean rí*, there being no word in the Irish language for a female ruler.

In 1574 an English force set sail from Galway and laid siege to Granuaile at Rockfleet. After many days she succeeded in turning defence into offence and the English were forced to flee ignominiously to avoid capture. Queen Elizabeth sent Sir Henry Sidney to Connacht in 1576 to demand submission from the Gaelic chieftains of the region, including the man who had replaced Dubhdarra as head of the clan Uí Máille. These submissions signalled the beginning of the end for the old Gaelic order in Connacht.

Granuaile was among those who appeared before Sidney. Afterward he wrote, 'There came to me also a most feminine sea captain called Grany Imallye, and offered her services unto me, wheresoever I would command her, with three galleys and 200 fighting men, either in Scotland or Ireland … This was a notorious woman in all the coasts of Ireland.'

While Granuaile appeared to submit, however, she was far from submissive. She was merely bowing to the political reality of the moment. She recognised that the power lay with the English and thought it best to appear to go along with them. But in reality, she would change sides if it suited her.

These were turbulent years for Granuaile. One of her sons, Owen O'Flaherty, was murdered in Ballinahinch Castle. His brother Murrough could not be relied upon to support his mother politically. Fortunately, her daughter Margaret's husband, who was known as 'The Devil's Hook', remained an ally. Granuaile also had her son Tibbot Burke to raise in an Ireland which was changing faster than anyone might have believed.

In 1584 Sir Richard Bingham was appointed Governor of Connacht. The province was far from pacified. Rebellion broke out repeatedly and Granuaile was often in the thick of it. She was at heart an unrepentant Gael who delighted in confounding the Sasanach – the English. Together with his brother John, Richard Bingham did everything he could to destroy Granuaile's power and influence. Twice he had her thrown into prison. Her property was confiscated, and many of her relatives and followers slain. Even her own son Murrough was used against her.

It seemed nothing could break her spirit. In a letter written by Richard Bingham in 1593 he describes Granuaile as 'a notable traitoress and nurse to all rebellions in the Province for 40 years'. That same year, however, she sent a letter to Queen Elizabeth, imploring the queen to settle upon her, from her late husbands' confiscated estates, a sum of 'reasonable maintenance' for the 'little time' she had left to live.

Burghley, the queen's private secretary, replied with 18 articles of interrogatory, closely questioning both her circumstances and the position of widows in Gaelic society. Her astute replies avoided many of the traps set out in the articles, while neglecting to mention her more outrageous exploits. But while she was awaiting an answer, Richard Bingham arrested her son, Tibbot.

Granuaile then undertook the most daring mission of her life. She sailed to Greenwich to confront Queen Elizabeth in person and plead not only her own cause, but that of her family. She was the first Gaelic woman ever to appear at the English court. Tales of the meeting between these two 'she-kings' are varied and colourful. They were about the same age; both were rulers of men. But one appeared wild and free while the other was imprisoned within her own ambitions.

Songs were sung, poems composed and portraits subsequently painted to show the striking differences between the two women. One thing appears certain: Elizabeth was impressed enough by Granuaile to grant her petition.

Granuaile sailed home to Ireland, but not yet into old age. Her galleys would continue to put to sea for some time to come. She remained physically active well into her sixties, running weapons for the rebellious Ulster noblemen Red Hugh O'Donnell and Hugh O'Neill.

Evidence suggests that she eventually died in bed at her beloved Rockfleet sometime around 1603 – the same year that saw the death of Queen Elizabeth I.

CHAPTER 3

Dónal Cam O'Sullivan Beare (c.1560–1618)

'The Last Prince'

The remote region known as the Beara peninsula at the south-western tip of Ireland is an area of rugged but breathtaking beauty. In the sixteenth century the dominant clan was O'Sullivan. They claimed descent from the fabled Iron-Age Milesians. The clan possessed a fine herd of cattle, but its primary income was from the sea. Their chieftain maintained a large fleet of trading vessels and fishing boats, several castles and a private army. Traditionally a portion of his income was owed to his overlord in the province of Munster, the MacCarthy Mór, but this scarcely diminished his prosperity. Hardy and self-reliant, his people had lived a free life for 1000 years and expected to continue for 1000 more.

In the latter half of the sixteenth century the clan produced a man of singular courage and determination. His nickname, Dónal Cam, reputedly referred to a crooked shoulder. Contemporary portraits do not reveal this. They depict a darkly handsome individual, aristocratic and almost Spanish in appearance, as one might expect of a descendant of Milesian nobility.

During this era the relentlessly encroaching English were having an effect on all aspects of Gaelic society as they attempted to complete the conquest of Ireland. When, in 1587, Dónal Cam challenged his uncle's right to the clan chieftaincy, he shrewdly bypassed the MacCarthy Mór and took his case directly to the English magistrate. After two years Dónal Cam was confirmed under English law as O'Sullivan Beare, Prince of Beara and Bantry, with the understanding that he would hold his lands thenceforth for Queen Elizabeth I.

In response to military pressure or outright bribery Irish chieftains had been making similar arrangements to save their lands and their lives since the reign of Henry VIII. This policy waas known as 'Surrender and Regrant'. If he surrendered himself and his tribal lands to the Crown, a chieftain was regranted part, though not all, of the land, and was given an English title. Gaelic chieftains were accustomed to native overlords in the form of provincial kings and high kings. To many of them, the English monarch was just one more and represented no threat to their traditional way of life.

O'Sullivan Beare remained neutral from the growing conflict in Ireland for some years, enjoying the prerogatives of chieftainship in his favourite castle at Dunboy, County Cork, as well as valuable trade with Elizabeth's merchant fleet. But an influx of English settlers into the fertile lands of southern Ireland was threatening the stability of the region. In 1600 the native Irish rose in revolt. Elizabeth I ordered Sir George Carew, whom she had named Lord President of Munster, to put down the rebellion. He obeyed with unparalleled savagery, laying waste to much of the province.

In the meantime two other members of the Gaelic nobility – Hugh O'Neill, Earl of Tyrone, and Red Hugh O'Donnell, Prince of Tyrconnell – were waging a campaign against the English in the northern province of Ulster. Their successes gave hope that

Ireland could be reclaimed from the foreigners. Some formerly uncommitted chieftains threw in their lot with O'Neill, who sought additional help from Catholic Spain, Queen Elizabeth's most feared enemy. Twelve years after the mighty Spanish Armada had sailed, another Spanish fleet set out for Ireland. Hugh O'Neill marched the length of the land to meet them.

In Munster O'Sullivan Beare's neutrality was wavering. As long as he remained loyal to Elizabeth he was safe from Carew, but that loyalty was only skin-deep, a matter of expediency. He was Gaelic to the bone. When Don Juan del Aguila arrived with the Spanish fleet at the southern port of Kinsale, O'Sullivan sent word that he was prepared to offer him 2000 soldiers to fight against the English. Half would be armed at O'Sullivan's expense; the remainder were to be armed by the Spanish. Del Aguila refused the offer.

However, the Spaniard did divide his fleet and send the smaller portion to Castlehaven on the Beara peninsula. Their arrival was enough to convince O'Sullivan Beare to join the rebellion openly. In a letter to Philip III of Spain he delivered his castle of Dunboy, his family and lands to the king's protection and pledged him his entire support in the struggle to come. Leaving Dunboy garrisoned by the Spaniards, O'Sullivan marched off to Kinsale to join O'Neill, O'Donnell and their allies.

On 24 December 1601, the Irish led by O'Neill confronted the English army under the command of Lord Mountjoy. The English were short of supplies and ill with dysentery, but the Irish threw away their advantage with quarrels over command and a lack of coordination of forces. Even so, had they received support from del Aguila's men they might have won. But the Spanish, safely garrisoned inside the walled town of Kinsale, appeared unaware of the battle.

At the end of the day, 1200 dead Irishmen lay on the battlefield and Mountjoy was victorious. Though the combatants did not realise it at the time, the Battle of Kinsale would prove to be the death knell of Gaelic Ireland.

O'Sullivan Beare was one of the few Irish leaders who managed to keep his head in the panic that followed defeat, and extricate his forces intact. O'Neill led what remained of his army back to Ulster, while O'Donnell set off for Spain to appeal to the king for more aid. Before departing, they appointed O'Sullivan commander of the army of Munster. It was not an enviable position.

O'Sullivan returned to the Beara peninsula and reclaimed Dunboy from the Spaniards. Dunboy was now the main rebel fortress in Munster, and its subjugation became a prime objective for Carew. The rugged terrain around the stronghold seemed to make it impenetrable. Carew brought cannon and soldiers by sea, then unexpectedly marched them overland while O'Sullivan was some miles away at Ardea, receiving much-needed supplies of food, ammunition and gold. Cannon breached the walls of Dunboy before O'Sullivan could return and the castle was destroyed.

A lesser man might have given up. Instead, O'Sullivan Beare gathered his surviving followers and their livestock and broke out of the trap the English had set for him on the Beara peninsula. A force under the command of Sir Charles Wilmot pursued them as far as Glengarriff on Bantry Bay, where Wilmot surrounded them and captured the clan's cattle. Over 1000 men, women and children were thus left without provisions in an exceptionally bitter winter.

O'Sullivan arranged for the weak and the wounded to remain behind as decoys, setting large fires to make Wilmot think all the Irish were still encamped. Then in the dead of the night he led the rest of his people away. The Great March had begun.

Their escape took Wilmot by surprise and he did not pursue them until too late. O'Sullivan's destination was O'Neill's camp on the shores of Lough Neagh in County Antrim, a distance of over 400 miles on foot. The route lay across mountains and rivers and through dense forests. Even in good weather and with adequate equipment, the journey would have been daunting.

O'Sullivan had to fight every step of the way, against not only the weather and the terrain and the English, but the Irish as well. Although he had gold, there was no food to buy in devastated Munster. The people whose territory he crossed attacked him in desperation to keep what little they had. In addition, Elizabeth's agents had put a price on his head. Many of the Irish sought to claim the reward and ingratiate themselves with the conquerors. Every day was a battle, and colder than the one before. Soon the ground was so frozen the refugees could no longer even bury their dead. Starving and on the verge of despair, they fled through a land where almost every man's hand was turned against them.

As the days passed, men and women lost strength and heart. Those who could go no further were given gold from O'Sullivan's own purse and allowed to stay behind. Some of them survived – and remembered. Their descendants are still scattered across Ireland, marking the trail with their genes.

A fortnight after leaving Glengarriff the survivors reached Leitrim. There Ó Ruairc of Breifne, a tribal kingdom which at its greatest height included parts of the current counties Sligo,

Leitrim, Roscommon, Westmeath and Meath, was still holding out against the English. Other fugitives had found sanctuary with him and he gladly took in what remained of clan O'Sullivan: 34 men, one woman – Dónal Cam's aunt – and the indomitable Dónal Cam himself.

After a brief period of rest and recuperation O'Sullivan raised fresh troops and set out once more in search of O'Neill. They would resume the fight, Ireland was not yet lost! He reached O'Neill's camp only to hear terrible news: O'Neill had already gone to Mellifont Abbey in County Meath to surrender formally to Mountjoy. It was over after all.

Some of the Irish chieftains were granted pardons and had their English titles restored, but not O'Sullivan Beare. He had become, in effect, the last Gaelic prince of Ireland. Because he had sworn allegiance to the King of Spain his lands were confiscated and himself exiled. He was in good company. Hugh O'Neill and his kinsmen were being forced to flee Ireland to save their lives. Their departure would become known as the Flight of the Earls.

O'Sullivan Beare made his way to Spain – where the daring Red Hugh had died at the age of 28, poisoned by agents of Carew. Dónal Cam was more fortunate. He was granted estates and an income and treated with every courtesy. For the rest of his life he did what he could to encourage ongoing resistance to the English domination of Ireland. When he died in Madrid in 1618 members of the Spanish royal family walked in his funeral procession.

CHAPTER 4

Owen Roe O'Neill (c.1590–1649)

'The Victorious Exile'

Owen Roe O'Neill was born into a clan noteworthy for famous rebels. Less than a generation after the collapse of the Geraldine resistance in Munster, Shane O'Neill had called Ulster to arms against the English in 1551. In 1601 Hugh O'Neill, who was Owen Roe's uncle, had led his people to battle once more.

Owen Roe took part in the Battle of Kinsale while he was still a very young boy. Afterward, as the victorious English systematically laid waste to the four provinces, Owen Roe left Ireland with the Flight of the Earls. Most of them would never see home again. Hugh O'Neill died of melancholia in Rome in 1616.

By then Owen Roe was fighting other battles in other lands. He became a military commander in the service of the King of Spain and acquitted himself with distinction in the Low Countries. At Arras in France – which as Nemetocenna had been one of the last Celtic strongholds to surrender to Caesar during the Gallic Wars – Owen Roe successfully held three armies at bay. But although Owen Roe O'Neill was loyal to the Spanish king, his heart remained with Ireland. He followed events there with interest.

After Kinsale, the victors had attempted to secure their conquest by establishing a highly repressive administration in Ireland, taking all aspects of government, patronage, power and land ownership into their own hands.

The majority of the population consisted of the native Gael. With their noble class destroyed or in exile, the demoralised peasants were leaderless. They had little choice but to accept what was done to them. A far more powerful group was the 'Old English', Catholic descendants of the twelfth-century Norman invaders. A third group, known as the 'New English', consisted of colonists and adventurers who had flocked to Ireland during the reign of the Tudors. The Old English, who by the seventeenth century were thoroughly Hibernicised, viewed this tightening governmental control as a threat. But the New English, inheritors of Tudor expansionism, recognised an unparalleled opportunity for land-grabbing.

From 1609 a great influx of Scottish and English settlers arrived in Ulster, displacing the natives. In return for the confiscated land they were given, these 'plantations' swore to hold Ulster for the Crown. English property law was rigidly enforced, invalidating Irish rights extending back for 1000 years. The extension of English power and influence in Ireland was further complicated by the matter of religion. The plantations were uncompromisingly Protestant.

The Irish were slowly recovering their will to freedom, however. An uprising began in Ulster on 22 October 1641, and spread through the province. The rebels were led by a lawyer, Sir Phelim O'Neill. Shortly after the rebellion began, Lord Lieutenant Chichester reported in a letter to King Charles I of England that the insurgents had taken four large towns but killed only one man so far. Yet in order to incite the extirpation of the Irish and provide still more land for covetous planters, a story was circulated to the effect that a 'fearful massacre of all the Protestants in Ireland' had taken place on the first night of the rising. Oliver Cromwell's secretary claimed that Irish Catholics had savagely murdered 610,000 Protestants – at a time when there were less than 200,000 Protestants in all of Ireland. It was the basest propaganda but many believed it, and no accurate figures were recorded in the State Papers. Thus were laid the foundations for hundreds of years of fear and hatred.

As the rising of 1641 gathered strength, King Charles and his parliament argued vehemently over who should have control of the army necessary to put down the rebellion. That argument ultimately led to Cromwell and parliament taking up arms against the monarch, and the start of the English Civil War in 1642.

Meanwhile, in Ireland, Sir Phelim was unable to sustain his early military successes. An experienced commander was needed and Owen Roe O'Neill, with a lifetime of successful battles behind him, was summoned with utmost urgency. One can imagine the joy with which he greeted the summons. He was no longer a young man, but here was the chance to fulfil the dream that had haunted him since he was a boy at Kinsale: the dream of rescuing Ireland.

In July 1642 Owen Roe O'Neill disembarked on the Donegal coast. Thanks to the magic of the O'Neill name he was able to raise a fresh army which he trained with consummate skill, inculcating military discipline into wild country lads. Over the next eight years Owen Roe would win numerous victories against the troops of the English government. The most famous of these took place at Benburb in County Donegal, when a superior enemy force was utterly destroyed through Owen Roe's brilliant tactics, with only 70 Irish killed.

During the 1640s Ireland became a tool in the war for hegemony being waged by the European powers. The French and Spanish governments sent envoys to Ireland promising support, but were more interested in recruiting Irish mercenaries to fight on the continent. The papacy also maintained an active diplomatic presence in Ireland. The country was torn between these Catholic interests and the political storms in England.

James Butler, Marquis of Ormond, was one of the most powerful men in Ireland at this time. Although by heredity he was 'Old English' – a descendant of the Catholic Normans – he had been reared in England and was virulently anti-Catholic. When Charles I found himself at odds with parliament, Ormond sided with the king and vowed to hold Ireland for him.

Ormond and his followers were part of an anti-Catholic coalition known as the Irish Royalists. Opposed to them was a Catholic association called the Confederation of Kilkenny, consisting of both clergy and laity and governed by a Supreme Council. The Confederation supported Owen Roe with men and weapons against Ormond. In a ferment composed of native Gael, Old and New English, Scots-English planters, Royalists, Parliamentarians, and the generally disaffected, Owen Roe O'Neill seemed the one bright light. As long as he could hold his forces together and stand like a rock, there was hope that Ireland might yet win back a degree of autonomy.

In 1647 Oliver Cromwell and his Parliamentarians defeated King Charles at Naseby in England, the first in a long row of defeats the English king was to suffer. Increasingly he sought help from his Irish supporters. The English Civil War ended in 1648 with a victory for the Parliamentarians, who put Charles on trial. On 30 January 1649, he was beheaded.

Within a matter of months Oliver Cromwell set sail for Ireland to crush the Royalists there. He arrived in August with 28 regiments. Upon landing in Dublin he took command of the city, then marched north to Drogheda, which was in Ormond's hands.

Cromwell left no doubt that he meant to subjugate all of Ireland as swiftly and brutally as possible. This was no time for faction fights. Owen Roe O'Neill, although in failing health, undertook an act of true statesmanship. He agreed to subordinate himself to Ormond's command and join in the defence of Drogheda. But the gesture came too late. As he was hurrying to Ormond's aid, Owen Roe fell ill and died in Cavan.

Without O'Neill's military genius, Ormond was unable to defend the city. The horrific massacre at Drogheda would become one of the most appalling chapters in Ireland's long history. The Cromwellian era had begun.

Theobald Wolfe Tone (1763–1798)

'The United Irishmen'

Theobald Wolfe Tone was born in Dublin in 1763, the grandson of a prosperous County Kildare farmer. His father was a successful coachmaker, his mother the daughter of a sea captain involved in the West India trade. She had been Catholic but eventually converted to the Anglican faith, the religion of her husband.

In eighteenth-century Ireland the Catholic majority was disenfranchised and the Protestant minority was divided. The ruling class consisted of Anglo-Irish Protestants known as the Ascendancy, members of the Anglican, or 'established' church. There was also a Protestant underclass of Scots Presbyterians, or 'Dissenters', the descendants of plantation colonists dating back to King James I's time. Many of these were prosperous landowners, but they were not allowed to take part in government or wield any real power.

Some form of parliament had been in existence in Ireland since 1541, when the King of England was also declared King of Ireland. Since 1707 England, Scotland and Wales had been joined in a polity calling itself Great Britain. The island of Ireland, in spite of almost constant effort by the English, had never been completely subdued, however. The British feared that their enemies might use

Ireland to launch an invasion force against them.

The origins of Irish Republicanism lie with the American and French revolutions. In 1776 the British had sent so many soldiers to the American colonies that there were not enough regular soldiers left to defend Ireland against a French or Spanish invasion. Therefore Britain sanctioned the formation of a volunteer militia charged with the defence of the island, and the first Volunteer Force was established in Ulster.

In France, Catholics were demonstrating that they could build a non-sectarian republic based on the ideals of liberty, equality and brotherhood. The Americans had already shown that freedom from English domination could be won through force of arms. By combining these two revolutionary examples with the existence of an armed militia, the Irish had the elements they would need for a revolution of their own.

In 1782 a band of militant Belfast Volunteers began protesting the discrimination suffered by Scots Presbyterians in Ulster. The Volunteer movement quickly spread throughout Ireland, attracting disaffected Protestants and Catholics alike.

Meanwhile, in 1781, Wolfe Tone had entered Trinity College, Dublin, where he spent much of his time in the pursuit of women. Four years later he eloped with Martha Witherington, a girl not quite 16 years old. Wolfe Tone re-named his bride 'Matilda', after a fictional ideal wife and mother. Now a family man with responsibilities, Wolfe Tone undertook the study of law and was called to the Bar in 1789. He did not much enjoy law, however, and soon turned his interest to politics, spending many hours in the galleries of the Irish Parliament. In the eighteenth century the Irish Parliament in Dublin was comprised of Ascendancy men, and was in effect a sub-division of the British Parliament.

A recent biographer claims that Wolfe Tone did not decry England as Ireland's enemy, but rather the disunity of the Irish themselves. However, in his autobiography Wolfe Tone tells us, 'I made speedily what was to me a great discovery: that the influence of England was the radical vice of our Government, and, consequently, that Ireland would never be either free, prosperous, or happy until she was independent, and that independence was unattainable whilst the connection with England existed.'

Although he belonged to the Ascendancy himself, Wolfe Tone further wrote of Ireland, 'Members of the established religion, though not above the tenth of the population, were in possession of the whole of the Government, and of five-sixths of the landed property of the nation. With properties whose title was founded in massacre and plunder, they saw no security for their persons and estates but in a close connection with England, who profited of their fears.'

Wolfe Tone soon became involved in agitation on behalf of oppressed Presbyterians and Catholics. In 1791, building upon a base of Volunteers, he helped found the United Irishmen. The new organisation was dedicated to breaking the ties with Britain by force. Again in Wolfe Tone's own words, its purpose was 'To unite the whole people of Ireland, to abolish the memory of all past dissensions, and to substitute the common name of Irishman in place of the Denominations of Protestant, Catholic, and Dissenter.' The United Irishmen considered a republic the best political structure for achieving this ideal.

Although much of the native population had no interest in politics and would not involve themselves in rebellion, the

British government reacted with alarm to the rapid growth of the revolutionary spirit in Ireland. A stringent Act of Insurrection was passed in 1795. In consequence Wolfe Tone and his family were forced into exile in America. While there he received letters from Ireland informing him that the enthusiasm for republicanism was growing, but outside help in the form of men and arms was desperately needed.

The United Irishmen felt their best chance would be an alliance with the French. Wolfe Tone decided to make the appeal in person, and in February of 1796 he set off for France. He was received courteously by the Directory, the ruling body of the new French Republic, with whom he was soon involved in protracted discussions.

Initially he was promised ten sailing vessels, any quantity of arms, and money. Wolfe Tone stressed that nothing could be accomplished except with the assistance of a French invasion force led by a general of established reputation. He drew up two elaborate presentations of his plans, which he called 'memorials' and presented them to various officials. Months went by without apparent progress. Wolfe Tone was increasingly frustrated by being stalled in what he perceived as a bureaucratic backwater. 'My time drags just now most horribly,' he wrote.

One of France's best generals, Lazare Hoche, was concluding a campaign in Brittany, and in June of 1796 Wolfe Tone was told of Hoche's prospective involvement in the Irish scheme. With renewed optimism, Wolfe Tone set about recruiting as many men as he could to assist in the invasion.

In Ireland one of his strongest supporters among the United Irishmen was Henry Joy McCracken, a Belfast-born man of

Huguenot ancestry. McCracken was arrested and imprisoned in Kilmainham Jail in Dublin for 13 months in 1796, but upon his release immediately went back to work for the cause. He was appointed to command insurgents in County Antrim when the rising began.

On 30 November 1796, Wolfe Tone prepared for embarkation himself and wrote a loving letter to his wife Matilda. A large invasion force set sail in the middle of December under the command of General Hoche on the *Fraternité*. Wolfe Tone was on board the *Indomptable*. To avoid the British fleet they took a route which proved disastrous. Fog and storms scattered the fleet. The flagship carrying Hoche was blown far out into the Atlantic. Thirty-six ships eventually reached Bantry Bay, where they were overtaken by another gale. The fleet was so badly battered that the attempt to land was abandoned and the survivors straggled back to France. But the British government had been warned. Preparations began in earnest to destroy any further hopes of revolution in Ireland.

Hoche also survived to return to France and resume his military career, but his star was being eclipsed by Napoleon Bonaparte. Wolfe Tone followed Hoche to Germany to try to resurrect the Irish invasion plans. Work continued throughout the year. A second expedition was being organised in spite of dissension among the various factions involved. Then in September of 1797 Hoche suddenly died. His death stunned the Irish and left them without their French champion.

Bonaparte succeeded Hoche and set out on an Egyptian campaign, but showed no interest in an Irish enterprise. Wolfe Tone would not give up. He made new friends and allies and continued to pressure France, as well as seeking aid in Holland.

In Ireland military purges were causing panic and an uprising was imminent, with or without foreign support. Then in May 1798 the long-awaited rebellion broke out. Wolfe Tone wrote, 'From the blood of every one of the martyrs of the liberty of Ireland will spring, I hope, thousands to revenge their fall.'

At last, in late summer, Wolfe Tone and another French expedition, much smaller than the first, set out for Ireland. By the time they arrived, however, they found that the rising had been all but crushed. Part of the fleet, under General Humbert, had landed in Killala Bay in County Mayo and enjoyed some brief successes against the British but then they had been decisively beaten. At this point, the rebellion collapsed. Meanwhile British warships attacked and seized the vessel containing Wolfe Tone, who fought valiantly to the end. He was arrested and thrown in irons, then taken to Dublin for court martial.

At about this same time, Henry Joy McCracken, whose attack on the British in Antrim had met with defeat, was being hanged in Belfast.

As a prominent member of the Protestant Ascendancy and a founder of the United Irishmen, and for having sided with France against Britain, Wolfe Tone was charged with high treason. His responses to the charges brought against him set a standard for Irish patriotic speeches. Summarily condemned, he was refused his request for a soldier's death. Instead he was to be hanged like a common felon. To thwart this final indignity he attempted suicide by cutting his throat. He did not die immediately, but lingered in agony for eight days. His friends applied for medical aid for him but this was denied. Wolfe Tone died on November 19 1798, and was buried in Bodenstown Cemetery in Dublin.

The immediate result of the failed 1798 Rising was the abolition of a separate Irish Parliament and the enforced Act of Union with Britain in 1800. Ireland as a nation was extinguished. But Theobald Wolfe Tone is remembered as the father of physical force republicanism, and more importantly as the prophet of a new and independent Ireland.

CHAPTER 6

Father John Murphy (1753–1798)

'The Rebel Priest'

The rising of 1798 involved a number of colourful individuals, but few have such a poignant hold on the Irish consciousness as Father Murphy, the Rebel Priest. The youngest son of a tenant farmer in County Wexford, John Murphy might be said to have represented the vast majority of Irish people of his era. His Gaelic ancestry extended back into the mists of pre-history and his roots were firmly planted in the soil.

Under the harsh Penal Laws in force in eighteenth- century Ireland, whose purpose was to keep the majority poor and disempowered, Catholic children were forbidden an education. Like so many others, John Murphy was educated in a 'hedge school'. Operating in secrecy, hedge schoolmasters taught the youngsters to read and do their sums, and often much more. Young John Murphy learned both Latin and Greek. These were of great benefit to him when he decided upon the priesthood.

Initially he studied with his Jesuit parish priest, Dr Andrew Cassin, and the Jesuitical approach further honed his mind. He also excelled in athletics and was an excellent horseman. After his ordination in 1799, Father Murphy elected to go to the Dominican College in Seville for further training. There he spent five years studying theology and philosophy and working with the large community of exiled Irish in the area.

When he returned to Ireland in 1785 he was given the curacy of Kilcormuck, County Wexford, an area better known as Boolavogue. Thanks to the power of music, 'Boolavogue' was the name which someday would make Father Murphy famous beyond the shores of Ireland.

Father Murphy celebrated Mass every morning beneath the thatched roof of Boolavogue chapel. He also rode many miles each week ministering to his parishioners, who grew to love the handsome and personable young priest. His life was pleasant, pastoral, familiar. But that life was on the verge of upheaval.

A new bishop, Dr James Caulfield, was posted to Wexford. Caulfield was determined to bring the traditional Catholic Church into line with what he saw as political reality. To this end he demanded an avowed transference of temporal loyalty on the part of his flock to King George III – a Protestant. Many of his parishioners found this unpalatable. Father Murphy loyally upheld his superior, though privately he may have begun to hold another opinion.

In 1791 Theobald Wolfe Tone, a young Protestant lawyer, helped to found the United Irishmen, whose aim was to bring people of all religious persuasions together in a democratic separatist movement dedicated to wide-reaching reforms.

In Wexford an intense recruiting drive was begun for the United Irishmen. Pamphlets explaining the organisation and its aims were handed out in the churchyards, including Boolavogue. Catholics responded with enthusiasm. The strains in the Church between liberal and conservative thinking began to show. Some priests openly supported the United Irishmen and suffered the scathing vituperation of Dr Caulfield. Thinking it best for the protection of his parishioners in Kilcormuck, Father Murphy encouraged them to sign a renewed pledge of loyalty to King George. This only elicited contempt from the government.

Soon all of Wexford was put under martial law. Loyalist militia were brought in to control the populace. They arrived with all the pomp and pageantry of British militarism and proceeded to abuse and torture men, women and children alike. One of the most brutal methods was 'pitch-capping', which involved filling a conical cap with boiling pitch and then pressing it down on the victim's head. Another pastime consisted of cropping a victim's hair, then applying moistened gunpowder to the scalp of the 'croppy' and setting it afire.

At first Father Murphy tried to gain clemency for his people by urging them to turn in their hidden weapons, but eventually he realised the situation was beyond control. Murder and farm-burnings were escalating dramatically and no attempt was being made to control militia terror gangs. By early in 1798, Kildare and Carlow were rumoured to be rising in revolt against similar mistreatment.

Wexford's United Irishmen determined to meet force with force. John Murphy had to make his own decision. These were his people who were being murdered. He chose to stand with them.

At night he carefully removed from Boolavogue chapel everything which might be desecrated, then, putting his vestments and few belongings into a bag, he threw in his lot with the rebels. He at first joined with 30 other men who were attempting to protect homes in the area. A very few had guns. Most were armed only with pikestaffs, pitchforks or slash hooks. And courage.

Their first encounter was with yeoman cavalry from nearby Camolin Barracks, who had come to burn out a local homestead and slaughter its inhabitants. The yeomen opened fire on Murphy and his companions but the Wexford men were ready for them. In a matter of minutes, two of the yeomen – one of them an officer and member of the gentry – lay dead. Father John Murphy was a full-fledged outlaw now, a rebel in arms against a monarch to whom he had sworn an oath of loyalty. There could be no going back.

Day by day, battle was joined throughout Wexford. At first the inexperienced rebels were unable to stand up to trained militia. But they soon learned. One of their ablest and most inspiring leaders was the formerly peaceful priest from Boolavogue. 'It would be better for us to die like men,' he is reported as having said, 'than to be butchered like dogs in the ditches. If I have any men to join me, I am resolved to sell my life dearly.'

At the Battle of Oulart Hill Father Murphy led a mixed band of insurgents. He had only 1000 fighting men, but there were also between 3000 and 4000 women, children and elderly people who had abandoned their homes in fear as 'redcoats' from the North Cork Militia approached. Father Murphy's pikemen attacked the militia with ferocity, taking terrible revenge for floggings and rapings and torture. The militiamen could not resist such passion; they broke and ran. Father Murphy collected their abandoned weapons, which were used in subsequent rebel victories at Ferns, Enniscorthy and Wexford town.

By June the government forces had adopted a policy of containment, with garrisons reinforced around the perimeter of the county. The rebel army had managed some thrilling victories, yet inexorably the tide began to turn against them. More and more troops were rushed to Wexford, which was seen as the heart of the rebellion. On 21 June the insurgents were overwhelmed and decisively defeated at Vinegar Hill.

The last flames of the rebellion of 1798 flickered out in July, with surviving Wexford rebels escaping to hide in the Wicklow Mountains. Civil and military authorities set about restoring order – which included savage retribution against the rebel Presbyterians in Ulster. Scores of them were tried and hanged.

Father Murphy and a companion were captured in County Carlow by yeoman farmers who wanted their horses. When they were searched, a small crucifix and a vial of oil for administering the Last Rites were found on John Murphy. That was all the evidence needed against him. He was bound and flogged. When he refused to cry out or divulge any information he was hanged in the market square of Tullow Town. As a last act of barbarity his head was cut from his body and carried in triumph through the town. It was finally impaled on a spike near the Catholic church to terrify the congregation. Father Murphy's torso was burned in a barrel of pitch. When only bone and ashes remained, they were thrown out on the ground and water was poured on the flames.

At Boolavogue, as the sun was setting

O'er soft May meadows of Shelmalier,

A rebel hand set the heather blazing

And brought the neighbours from far and near.

Then Father Murphy from old Kilcormuck

Spurred up the rocks with a warning cry:

'Arm, arm!' he cried, 'For I come to lead you,

For Ireland's freedom we fight or die!

CHAPTER 7

Robert Emmet (1778–1803)

'The Darling of Erin'

Robert Emmet belongs to the pantheon of Protestant patriots who were willing to fight and die for Irish freedom. He was born in Dublin, the son of Dr Robert Emmet, an eminent Dublin physician whose Kerry-born wife, Eileen Mason, bore her husband 18 children. Five of them were named after the doctor, but only the last survived infancy. Even among prosperous families such statistics were not uncommon in eighteenth-century Ireland.

When Robert was a boy, Wolfe Tone was a frequent visitor to the Emmet home. Robert's elder brother Thomas Addis Emmet, who was his senior by 14 years, was impressed by Tone and became deeply involved with the United Irishmen. Meanwhile, as a member of the Protestant Ascendancy, young Robert was being educated in the best private schools. In 1793 he was admitted to Trinity College, where he distinguished himself in the Historical Society. A bright future was predicted for him.

While still in TCD Robert Emmet also joined the United Irishmen. In 1798 the Lord Chancellor visited the college to learn the extent of student support for the organisation, and Emmet was one of the young men summoned before him. Emmet felt he was being treated like a criminal. This so outraged him that he struck his name from the college rolls, ruining his chances of a professional career.

From that moment his course was set. For the next several years he threw his heart into the cause of Irish nationalism to such an extent that an arrest warrant was issued for him. Before it could be enforced he travelled to the Continent and joined his brother Thomas there.

Thomas Addis Emmet had also been educated at TCD before studying medicine at Edinburgh University. He had switched to law and been called to the Irish Bar in 1790. His practice mostly consisted of nationalists; he was one of the advisors to the United Irishmen during the 1798 Rising. He was arrested in March of that year but released into exile. As agent for the United Irishmen he then travelled to Brussels and Paris, once more seeking promise of an expeditionary force to aid an Irish revolution.

When Robert Emmet joined Thomas in France, the two made an effort to gain a commitment from the government. Among those with whom they spoke was Napoleon Bonaparte. Napoleon showed little interest, being preoccupied with the simmering situation with England. But there were offers of help from the Directory, in the form of men and arms that would be sent as soon as a rising began. Encouraged by this, Robert Emmet returned to Dublin in March of 1803, to gather the survivors of 1798 and start again. He was further promised support by influential persons in Ireland, particularly in the North.

Emmet's main work was concentrated in Dublin, however. He negotiated the lease on a house in Butterfield Lane, Rathfarnham, under the assumed name of Ellis. From here he developed a network consisting of a number of nationalists in the eastern region. These included one Bernard Duggan of Kildare, a spy in the pay of the British government.

Working at fever pitch, the ardent Emmet recruited men and established arms depots in and around Dublin. In the meantime he secretly became engaged to Sarah Curran, the daughter of his friend and mentor, the lawyer John Philpot Curran. The couple found privacy for their courting at the Hermitage in Rathfarnham, a country estate in the foothills of the Dublin Mountains, and close to Sarah's own home. When Sarah's favourite horse died it was buried in the grounds at the Hermitage. Years later, the estate became the home of Patrick Pearse's famous school, Saint Enda's.

John Philpot Curran was a strong Irish nationalist and opponent of the Act of Union, and had defended Wolfe Tone after the 1798 Rising. In spite of this, when he learned of his daughter's romance with Robert Emmet, Curran was furious. He resented the clandestine nature of the romance and felt that the relationship could put himself in some danger. His treatment of his daughter was so unreasonable that she fled her home. For a time she took refuge with friends in Cork.

Broken-hearted, Robert Emmet went ahead with his plans for a rising. One of his staunchest allies was a young woman called Anne Devlin, who shared his dream of Irish independence. She masqueraded as his housekeeper while carrying messages for the conspirators.

When Britain resumed war with France in 1803, Emmet planned his rising to begin in Dublin at the same time as an anticipated August invasion of England by Napoleon. But he was badly overstretched; if anything went wrong, he was in trouble. And something did go very wrong.

On 16 July explosives in Emmet's arms depot in Patrick Street ignited and killed a workman there, alerting the authorities. Emmet felt there was no choice but to go ahead as soon as possible, and until such a time, he lived at another arms depot in Marshalsea Lane, where he had 3000 pikes, 12 cases of pistols, four muskets and 18 blunderbusses.

Emmet's planned uprising was doomed from the start. The help he expected from outside Dublin failed to arrive. His officers quarrelled; his troops were ill-prepared and confused. With every passing hour the situation grew more desperate. On the evening of 23 July 1803, Robert Emmet donned a green-and-gold uniform of his own design and set out from Marshalsea Lane at the head of 100 overexcited, undisciplined men. Their intention was to attack Dublin Castle, the seat of British authority in Ireland.

On their way to Dublin Castle the company encountered a coach containing Arthur Wolfe, the Lord Chief Justice, and his nephew. Wolfe was a kind-hearted old man who had tried to help Wolfe Tone. However, some of the rebels mistook Wolfe for the so-called 'hanging judge', Lord Norbury. They dragged the two men from the coach and, before Emmet could prevent it, killed them both with pikes. Then they ran amok. With his plans in shambles, Robert Emmet fled to the Wicklow Mountains and went into hiding.

His ally Michael Dwyer – who had failed to show up when Emmet summoned him for the rising – urged that neighbouring towns be attacked to draw out the British. But Emmet refused to risk any more lives until the promised foreign aid arrived. He dispatched a message to his brother Thomas in Paris pleading with the French to send help at once. They never did, of course.

During this time Robert Emmet was shielded and protected by the faithful Anne Devlin. On one occasion, yeomen searching Emmet's house in Rathfarnham tortured Anne Devlin to make her reveal his whereabouts. When the heroic young woman refused to tell what she knew, she was thrown into prison.

While he was in hiding Robert Emmet's thoughts returned again and again to Sarah Curran. Unable to resist an overpowering desire to see his sweetheart once more, he arranged to meet her at Harold's Cross in Dublin. An informer revealed the plan to the British. An officer called Major Sirr was waiting for Emmet at Harold's Cross when he arrived. The young man was arrested and thrown into Kilmainham Jail. Unknown to him, Anne Devlin was in a cell almost directly beneath his, embarking on an imprisonment which was to last three years and destroy her health.

Emmet was tried in front of Lord Norbury – the infamous hanging judge. Emmett's lawyer, a man called MacNally, promptly told the prosecution everything he had learned in confidence from his client. Emmet was convicted. When Norbury asked if he had anything to say before sentence was passed, Emmet delivered an oration from the dock that earned him immortality.

Let no man write my epitaph; for as no man who knows my motives dare now vindicate them, let not prejudice or ignorance disperse them. Let them rest in obscurity and peace, my memory left in oblivion, and my tomb remain uninscribed until other men can do justice to my character. When my country takes her place among the nations of the world, then, and only then, let my epitaph be written.

On 20 September 1803, Robert Emmet was executed in front of St Catherine's Church in Thomas Street. He mounted the scaffold with a firm step. After he was hanged, his head was cut off and jeeringly displayed to the crowd as that of a traitor to Ireland. He was 24 years old.

CHAPTER 8

Daniel O'Connell (1775–1847)

'The Liberator'

Daniel O'Connell was a statesman who espoused nationalism without violence. His cradle was the kingdom of Kerry, that stern but spectacularly beautiful region at the southwest corner of Ireland. O'Connell's grandfather was called Dónal Mor O'Connell; his grandmother was known as Máire Ní Dhuiv – Mary of the Dark Folk. Young Daniel's father, Morgan, farmed and ran a general store near Cahirciveen, and his mother, Catherine, was a daughter of the 'Chief of the Name' of the Mullane clan.

From this romantic Gaelic background, Daniel's life took a number of unexpected turns. When he was not yet six he was adopted by his prosperous Uncle Maurice, known as 'Hunting Cap'. A shrewd businessman, Hunting Cap could not own property or conduct business dealings openly because he was a Catholic, so he worked through Protestant contacts.

During the ten years that Daniel lived with his uncle, he obtained his education through the good offices of hedge schoolmasters. When Daniel proved himself something of a prodigy, he was sent to Cork for more formal schooling. In 1791 he was sent to the Continent for further education.

In France he was taken under the wing of another relative,

Right: Thomas
FitzGerald, Lord
Offaly and 10th Earl of
Kildare (1513–1537).
Below: Granuaile (on
left) (c.1530–1603).

Right: Dónal Cam O'Sullivan Beare (c.1560–1618).
Below: Owen Roe O'Neill (1590–1649).

Right: Theobald Wolfe
Tone (1763–1798).
Below: Father John
Murphy (1753–1798).

Left: Robert Emmet
(1778–1803).
Below: Daniel
O'Connell (1775–1847)

Top left: William Smith O'Brien (1803–1864).
Top right: John Mitchel (1815–1875).
Left: James Connolly (1868–1916).

Right: Countess Constance Markievicz (1868–1927).
Below: James Larkin (1876–1947).

Top left: Patrick Pearse
(1879–1916).
Above: Terence MacSwiney,
Lord Mayor of Cork
(1879–1920).
Bottom left: Michael Collins
(1890–1922).

Above: Bobby Sands
(1954–1981).
Right: Gerry Adams
(1948–).

Colonel Daniel Charles O'Connell, one of the Wild Geese who had fled Ireland to fight in foreign wars. Hunting Cap begrudgingly provided funds for Daniel's upkeep, even after they fled to London to avoid the turmoil of the French Revolution. In the years that followed, young Daniel would acquire a great deal of practice in conciliation and negotiation while extracting money from his increasingly wealthy – and increasingly penurious – Uncle Maurice in Kerry. Money was necessary to support Daniel in his ambition to become a lawyer. He entered Lincoln's Inn in 1794 and was called to the Bar in 1798.

During the 1798 rebellion Uncle Maurice, who was a supporter of the Crown, was one of those to warn the British of the impending uprising. Daniel O'Connell's feelings took a different turn. In his journal he wrote, 'Liberty is in my bosom less a principle than a passion ... but Ireland is not yet sufficiently enlightened to bear the sun of liberty.' Yet while he sympathised with the United Irishmen he did not join them in action. Instead he returned to Kerry.

His uncle had chosen a wife for him, but Daniel was his own man. When he fell in love with a distant cousin, Mary O'Connell of Tralee, a secret marriage was arranged. A son was born whom they named Maurice in an attempt to conciliate Hunting Cap, but the ploy failed. The furious old man threatened to disinherit his nephew.

O'Connell was forced to rely on his legal income to support his family. Catholic barristers were excluded from what was called the Inner Bar. Only moneyed Protestants could aspire to the prestigious title of King's Counsel and the fees the title commanded. But O'Connell possessed an exceptional talent for the law. While he was still in London members of the Inner Bar had often sought his help in their most difficult cases.

In Ireland at first his income came from 'circuit riding' – representing country people throughout the west and southwest. Known as the poor man's lawyer, O'Connell demonstrated a gift for oratory that enabled him to dominate juries and judges. His success was such that, in spite of charging nominal fees, he was eventually able to establish a practice in Dublin at the Four Courts.

Yet he continued circuit riding as well. He put his awesome energy and powerful intellect at the disposal of impoverished peasants who had run afoul of the system. These years of dedication gained him the admiration of the common people, an admiration that would later support him in public life. He was, for his time, a revolutionary thinker, advocating religious freedom and the complete separation of church and state. He also achieved an astonishing, and perhaps exaggerated, reputation for womanising. This only enhanced his aura.

In 1815 O'Connell ridiculed Dublin Corporation for its 'beggarly attitude'. He was challenged to a duel by a member of the Corporation, Norcot d'Esterre. Although he detested violence O'Connell accepted the challenge – and fatally wounded his opponent. Grief-stricken, he settled a pension on d'Esterre's widow and vowed that never again would he consent to the shedding of a single drop of human blood, except his own.

The Act of Union in 1800 had contained passages which had raised hopes for Catholic Emancipation – the right of Catholics to vote – but this had failed to materialise. O'Connell became interested in the struggle. In 1823 he founded the Catholic Association to employ all possible constitutional means for gaining emancipation for the Irish majority. In 1828 O'Connell ran for public office on the emancipation platform and won an overwhelming victory. The country was wildly excited. Fearing there would be another rising, the British reluctantly granted Catholic Emancipation.

Daniel O'Connell's reward was the emotional leadership of Ireland. He gave up his law practice to devote his entire time to politics. A special collection called the 'O'Connell Tribute' was taken up to compensate him for his sacrifice as he undertook the task of obtaining repeal of the Act of Union and achieving a representative parliament for the Irish people.

O'Connell believed his goals were reasonable and could be obtained through political methods. However Britain, which was still smarting from the loss of America in 1776, feared a repeal of the Act of Union would lead to an independent Ireland. This would mean the humiliating loss of one of England's earliest colonies, which would in turn make her more vulnerable to invasion. It simply could not be allowed. The Coercion Act, empowering local authorities to impose curfews and detention without trial, was introduced to thwart O'Connell's efforts.

The British government was unstable during this period, which added to its anxieties. Simultaneously, a movement known as the Young Irelanders was rekindling the separatist vision. Irish independence began to seem more than a hopeless dream.

The Repeal Association was founded by Daniel O'Connell on 15 April 1840, to focus his campaign for repeal of the Union between Great Britain and Ireland. In 1841 Daniel O'Connell was elected Lord Mayor of Dublin and began to organise 'monster meetings' throughout the country. It was estimated that three-quarters of a million people gathered on the Hill of Tara to hear the man they called 'the Liberator' speak of freedom.

The government was alarmed. On his way to another monster meeting in 1843, O'Connell was arrested and charged with conspiracy. He spent three months in prison before the House of Lords set the verdict aside. O'Connell, although he was almost 70, returned to the fight for repeal of the Union. A widower by now, he also became passionately enamoured of a young Protestant woman. His five sons and three daughters by his late wife were greatly embarrassed, but O'Connell's gusto for life remained undiminished.

However, there was a new enemy on the horizon. The Great Famine, which began in 1845, brought the Irish peasantry to unplumbed depths of human misery. The common people, who had always been O'Connell's strongest supporters, did not have enough energy left to fight for a dream when every waking hour was spent fighting to survive.

In 1847 a worn but unrepentant Daniel O'Connell made one last speech in the House of Commons. Then he left for Rome, where he wished to die. But in this he was thwarted. Daniel O'Connell died in Genoa on 15 May. His Catholic heart was sent on to Rome; his body was returned to Ireland and buried in a vault at Glasnevin Cemetery.

O'Connell had won Catholic Emancipation but failed to repeal the Act of Union. Yet he had won another, more enduring victory. He had shown the ordinary Irish people what they might achieve with a strong leader.

CHAPTER 9

William Smith O'Brien (1803–1864)

'The Cabbage Patch War'

Born at Dromoland Castle in County Clare, William O'Brien was the second son of Sir Edward O'Brien, a descendant of the great Brian Ború. William's mother was the former Charlotte Smith, whose father owned property in County Limerick. When William inherited the Limerick property he also added Smith to his surname in tribute to his mother. His was a proud Protestant family; his elder brother Lucius restored an ancient disused title and eventually became the 13th Baron Inchiquin.

William was born with the proverbial silver spoon in his mouth. A member of the landlord class, he was educated at Harrow and at Trinity College, Cambridge, before deciding on a political career. He entered national politics in 1828 as conservative Member of Parliament for the borough of Ennis. In 1832 he married Lucy Gabbett of High Park, County Limerick, who bore him five sons and two daughters. In 1835 he was re-elected to parliament as MP for Limerick.

O'Brien's experiences in parliament dramatically diminished his conservatism. Soon he was championing relief of the aged poor and the encouragement of elementary education for all. An enlightened Protestant who supported Catholic Emancipation, by 1844 O'Brien had joined Daniel O'Connell's Repeal Party, whose aim was the dismantling of the Act of Union. He became O'Connell's chief aide and then the movement's leader during the time O'Connell was imprisoned. Relations between the two men did not remain harmonious however, and they disagreed over matters of policy.

When a new nationalist organisation called the Young Irelanders was founded O'Brien joined at once, thus widening the breach between himself and O'Connell. The Young Irelanders wanted to keep religion out of politics, whereas O'Connell regarded Ireland's cause as inseparable from Catholicism.

The year 1847 was the height of the Great Famine in Ireland. Peasants were dying by the tens of thousands, unnecessarily and in the most appalling conditions. In parliament in London, O'Brien drew the attention of the House of Commons to Ireland's plight as often as possible. At home at Dromoland his brother Sir Lucius was making similar efforts. Both men were heartsick at the results of British policy in Ireland. But while Sir Lucius remained within the establishment, his younger brother would not. He was well on his way to becoming a gentleman revolutionary.

In March of 1848 O'Brien addressed a hostile parliament for the last time, warning that if repeal of the Union continued to be refused, 'You will encounter the chance of a republic in Ireland.' Shortly thereafter, at a public meeting in Dublin, O'Brien urged the formation of an Irish National Guard based on the militia that was an integral part of the new French Republic. He also advocated establishing a national parliament entirely independent of the United Kingdom. The revolutionary overtones were obvious. Leading Young Irelanders O'Brien and Thomas Meagher were arrested on charges of sedition. However, the government made the mistake of allowing Catholics onto the juries, which refused to convict. Both men had to be released.

During the weeks that followed O'Brien toured Ireland trying to rally support for a rising. Aware of these activities, the British sent over large numbers of additional military personnel. In addition the Catholic Church, fearful of being stripped of the prerogatives it retained, was vocal in its opposition to the outbreak of Irish nationalism.

Meanwhile an even more militant member of the Young Irelanders, the firebrand John Mitchel, had been arrested. His outspoken fearlessness at his trial added fuel to the flames. When he was deported the Young Irelanders could no longer contain themselves. With little preparation and no hope of success, they staged an uprising out of sheer frustration.

On 29 July 1848, a party of between 40 and 50 insurgents led by William Smith O'Brien approached the village of Ballingarry in County Tipperary. On the road they encountered a force of about the same number of policemen. With more discretion than valour, the police rushed for the safety of the nearest cottage. This belonged to Widow McCormack, who had gone to the village to shop and left her children at home alone. Wedging the widow's mattresses into the windows, the police barricaded themselves inside the house. The rebels – including both men and women armed with elderly firearms, pikes and agricultural implements – surrounded the cottage and its adjoining cabbage patch.

O'Brien walked up to the cottage, shook hands with one of the constables through an opening between a mattress and a window frame, and tried to persuade them to surrender. They refused. In hopes of smoking them out, the crowd set fire to some hay and piled it against the door. At this point an hysterical Mrs McCormack returned and protested the danger to her children and property.

While O'Brien was still trying to negotiate a surrender, a volley of stones provoked the police to fire. The rebels fired back as long as their limited ammunition lasted. One or two men were killed outright and several others injured. The crowd then ran, leaving O'Brien alone in the cabbage patch to face the furious Widow McCormack. He vaulted onto a police horse and galloped off.

The Young Irelanders' rebellion was over.

A week later William Smith O'Brien was arrested at Thurles station as he attempted to board one of the new railway trains. He was tried and convicted of high treason. Until conviction he was still a Member of Parliament, so although as punishment for high treason he was to be hanged, decapitated and quartered, in October his sentence was commuted to transportation. The British believed the safest place for rebels was thousands of miles away from Ireland, so he was sent to the penal colony of Van Diemen's Land, now known as Tasmania.

O'Brien spent five years in exile in Tasmania. In 1853 further transportation to the penal colony was abolished as a result of agitation by Tasmanian residents, who sympathised with their unwilling Irish guests. Meanwhile, in Ireland, Sir Lucius O'Brien and influential friends were making strenuous efforts to obtain a pardon for William. This was finally granted in May of 1854 with the condition that O'Brien never return to any part of the United Kingdom of Britain and Ireland.

He settled in Brussels with his wife and family, and spent

the next ten years travelling, lecturing and writing. He took no further part in politics and even disavowed his earlier flirtation with violence, so that in 1856 he was granted an unconditional pardon.

In 1864, whilst visiting his sister in North Wales, William Smith O'Brien died. His body was returned to Dublin where it received a hero's welcome. *The Nation* estimated the crowd accompanying the body from the docks to the railway station numbered 20,000. O'Brien was buried at Rathronan, near his County Limerick home. Today his statue may be seen in Dublin's O'Connell Street, not far from that of 'the Liberator'.

CHAPTER 10

John Mitchel (1815–1875)

'Jail Journal'

John Mitchel was born in what was then County Londonderry – a name the British had imposed on ancient Derry, from the Irish 'Daire', meaning oak. Mitchel's father, a Protestant minister, was also a member of the United Irishmen. John's early education took place in Londonderry and then in Newry, County Down, but he was subsequently sent to Trinity College in Dublin to study law. At that time only male Protestants could attend the prestigious college, founded during the reign of Elizabeth I of England.

When Mitchel's studies were completed he returned to Newry and went to work in a solicitor's office there. But his bright future was soon dimmed by scandal. In 1836 he ran away to England with a 16-year-old girl, Jane Verner. Mitchel was brought back to Ireland in disgrace and in custody, but unrepentant. The couple eloped again the following year and this time succeeded in marrying.

Mitchel began practising as a solicitor in the town of Banbridge in County Down in 1840. He made frequent visits to Dublin, however, and it was during one of these that he met a young Protestant barrister and poet, Thomas Davis, and his friend, Charles Gavan Duffy, a journalist. These men shared the vision of Irish independence which Mitchel had inherited from his father. When in 1842 Davis and Duffy began publishing a patriotic weekly called *The Nation*, Mitchel became a contributor.

The Nation was a huge success, with a readership that soon reached 250,000. Its emotive articles and essays and rousing patriotic ballads touched the hearts of those who had been inspired by Daniel O'Connell. There was a younger generation emerging which was equally excited by the philosophy behind *The Nation*, and had the energy to take up where O'Connell left off. From among them Davis brought together a group known as the Young Irelanders, whose goal was to work toward national independence. The Young Irelanders attracted the finest minds in the country, including such men as William Smith O'Brien and John Mitchel.

When the brilliant Davis died young in 1845, Duffy took over his mantle as a spokesman for separatism. He also asked John Mitchel to join the staff of the newspaper. Mitchel proved a great asset; his descriptions of areas devastated by the potato famine of 1845–1849 were particularly harrowing and made a vivid impression.

Duffy and many of his colleagues felt that Ireland was not yet ready to seek its freedom from the British Empire. The impoverished Irish, untrained and ill-equipped, would be bound to lose any military engagement. Furthermore, they were unprepared for self-government. Instead of advocating immediate rebellion, *The Nation* suggested the country must be 'ripened' into revolution, so the Irish people could confront the British from a position of relative strength.

John Mitchel did not share this viewpoint. He was impatient of temporising and the cautious approach. If Ireland waited to be strong, he argued, Britain would guarantee that she was kept weak forever. In 1848 Mitchel left *The Nation* and founded a paper called *The United Irishman*. From its first issue the newspaper preached armed rebellion. Although Mitchel advocated passive resistance for small farmers whose lives and property were under threat, if this should fail, as it inevitably would, he urged them to take up arms against the authorities. To aid in this he gave weekly instruction in pike practice. The classes were immensely popular.

In a very short time the readership of *The United Irishman* surpassed that of *The Nation*. Such a highly visible and defiant rebel could not be long ignored. Mitchel was arrested – shortly after the arrests of fellow Young Irelanders Meagher and O'Brien for sedition.

The authorities did not make the same error with John Mitchel which they had made with the other two. For him they invented a new crime, treason-felony, and were careful to ensure that only Protestants of a strong loyalist viewpoint were on the jury. From the dock Mitchel the polemicist made a powerful statement condemning packed juries and perjured testimony, but to no avail. He was convicted and sentenced to deportation to Tasmania. His friends contemplated attempting a rescue but decided against it because of the risk of killing innocent people.

Mitchel had hoped that his arrest and exile would provoke an insurrection that could lead on to freedom, but in this he was disappointed. The strongest protest was William Smith O'Brien's skirmish in County Tipperary, which was soon put down.

But Mitchel himself could not be silenced. In 1853 he escaped to America. There he published his *Jail Journal*, which attracted wide attention and brought the struggle in Ireland into sharp focus for American readers. The *Jail Journal* became a classic of prison literature. Among its pages was a statement to the effect that the Crimean War could be a blessing for Ireland, because it would keep Britain preoccupied and allow another rising to succeed.

Others were also seeking advantage for Ireland. In 1858 another Young Irelander, James Stephens, helped found a secret society known as the Fenian Brotherhood, and later as the Irish Republican Brotherhood (IRB). Appearing almost simultaneously in America and Ireland, the organisation advocated armed revolution. Irish-Americans flocked to join, building up both a political and an economic power base which had never been available before. This was to have far-reaching implications for the future of Ireland.

John Mitchel did not involve himself with the new society. Journalism was as deep in his bones as rebellion, and its call was irresistible. In America he founded several short-lived newspapers, then became editor of the *Richmond Examiner*. The outbreak of America's Civil War found him championing the Southern cause, seeing it as analogous to that of Ireland against the more powerful and industrialised England. Three of Mitchel's sons served in the Confederate Army; the eldest and youngest were killed in action.

After the war ended Mitchel continued to argue the South's case until he was imprisoned for several months by an exasperated Federal Government. In 1867 he founded yet another newspaper, the *Irish Citizen*, in New York. Controversial as ever, he infuriated American Fenians by insisting that they owed their allegiance to their new country.

This was not advice he took for himself. In 1874 he returned to Ireland to stand for election as Member of Parliament for Tipperary. The British authorities declared him ineligible because he was a convicted felon. Undaunted, Mitchel renewed his campaign – and the people enthusiastically swept him into office.

It was to be his last victory. John Mitchel died the following year in Newry, County Down, and was buried in the Unitarian Cemetery in High Street.

CHAPTER 11

James Connolly (1868–1916)

'We Serve Neither King Nor Kaiser'

James Connolly was a new sort of rebel for Ireland – a working-class rebel. He was born in Cowgate, an Edinburgh slum, to Irish immigrant parents from County Monaghan. Thanks to this parentage Connolly would always consider himself an Ulsterman.

Typically for the time, young James was sent out to work at 11 years of age. In 1882 he falsified his age in order to enlist in the British Army. Stationed in Ireland in 1889, a year later he deserted the army in order to marry Lillie Reynolds, a Protestant domestic servant from Carnew, County Wicklow. The young couple ran away to Scotland.

In Edinburgh, Connolly found work as a carter and became involved in trade union activities, which led to a lifelong devotion to socialism. As one of the pioneers of the modern labour movement in Edinburgh, he was active in both the Scottish Socialist Federation and the Independent Labour Party. The Scottish socialist movement drew inspiration from the writings of Karl Marx, which would prove an important influence on Connolly. When he lost his job in Scotland he became a paid organiser for the Dublin Socialist Club in 1896. In 1898 Connolly launched a weekly newspaper called the *Workers' Republic*, which was Ireland's first socialist newspaper.

A man of enormous energy, in 1896 he also founded the Irish Socialist Republican Party (IRSP) and served as its first secretary. The stated aim of the new party was to secure the national and economic freedom of the Irish people. Connolly used the centenary of the 1798 rebellion to espouse the principles of Wolfe Tone and argue that they could only be achieved in a socialist republic. The ISRP was plagued with internal difficulties, however, and never gained the wide base of support Connolly hoped for.

Meanwhile he was making a name for himself both as a journalist and a lecturer. Connolly toured Britain and America in 1902, giving lectures on political philosophy and the trade union movement. In 1903, when he found himself unable to make an adequate living in Ireland or Scotland, Connolly emigrated to America with his growing family. They were to remain in the United States for seven years, during which time Connolly had an opportunity to study American socialism at first hand. He worked with Daniel De Leon's Socialist Labour Party until, disagreeing with De Leon's 'sectish' tendencies, he broke away to help found the International Workers of the World in 1905.

In 1907, the year his daughter Fiona was born, Connolly organised the Irish Socialist Federation in New York. Its monthly journal, *The Harp*, was a platform for his own views. Connolly continued to think of himself as an Irishman, and in 1910 brought his family back to Ireland. He joined the Socialist Party of Ireland, which was the successor to the ISRP, and continued writing about socialist issues. His treatise *Labour, Nationality and Religion* defended the right of a Catholic to be a socialist. He also published *Labour In Irish History*, which described the working class as 'the incorruptible inheritors of the fight for freedom in Ireland'.

In 1911 Connolly took the step which was to lead him irrevocably to rebellion. He became Ulster organiser for the Irish Transport and General Workers' Union (ITGWU), founded by James Larkin. In 1913 Larkin was imprisoned following riots in Dublin during what became known as the Great Lock-Out. Connolly forced the government to release Larkin by effectively closing the port of Dublin.

That was the year Sir Edward Carson, leader of the Unionist Party, resurrected the eighteenth-century concept of a volunteer militia. His Ulster Volunteer Force (UVF) was not the organisation that had supported Wolfe Tone's ideal of a non-sectarian republic, however. The new UVF was a heavily armed Protestant organisation, sworn to prevent Home Rule, a form of limited self-government for Ireland. If the British government allowed the island of Ireland to have Home Rule, a democratically elected legislature would have put Catholics in the majority in the power structure for the first time since the Elizabethan conquest. Sir Edward Carson said No.

Provided with a vast array of weapons imported from both England and Germany, the UVF paraded through the streets of Belfast shouting anti-Catholic slogans. The threat of armed violence worked; the British government postponed Home Rule indefinitely.

Meanwhile Connolly and his family had settled in Dublin, and Larkin and Connolly were engaged in forming their own militia: the Irish Citizen Army. Its headquarters was Liberty Hall, the home of the Transport Workers' Union. The Citizen Army was dedicated to protecting workers from organised police brutality such as that displayed during the Great Lock-Out. Because Connolly was a strong believer in equality for women, the Citizen Army included female members. They drilled in Croydon Park alongside the men, using hurley sticks and wooden batons as weapons. James Connolly wrote, 'Fighting spirit is of more importance than the creation of the theoretically perfect organisation.'

In 1914 Larkin left for America to raise badly needed additional funds for the ITGWU. Connolly became acting secretary of the union, as well as Commandant of the Citizen Army. He was also editing a socialist newspaper, the *Irish Worker*. Connolly believed capitalism, with its heavy focus on a materialistic society, to be the enemy of peace and social justice. When war broke out in Europe in 1914, Connolly declared, 'We have no foreign enemy except the Government of England. We serve neither King nor Kaiser, but Ireland.' With these ringing words he committed the Irish labour union movement to opposing the war. As a result the *Irish Worker* was suppressed by the government. Undaunted, James Connolly started a new paper, the *Workers' Republic*.

But the Great War, as it was to be called, had a wider meaning for Ireland. Irish nationalists had long prophesied that England's difficulties would be Ireland's opportunity. The Irish Republican Brotherhood recognised that the time had come.

A nationalist organisation to counter the UVF had been founded in Dublin in 1914: the Irish National Volunteer Corps. Compared with the UVF the new militia was ill-trained and severely under-equipped, but what they lacked in materials they made up in enthusiasm. The IRB undertook to infiltrate the new Volunteers (without the knowledge of Eoin MacNeill and the other Volunteer leaders) bringing organisational skills and funding.

The nationalist movement was acquiring muscle.

Connolly disdained the Volunteers, not only as a rival force to his Citizen Army but as an anachronism. 'When are you fellows going to stop blethering about *dead* Fenians?' he demanded to know. 'Why don't you get a few live ones for a change?'

Little did he realise.

Unbeknown to both Connolly and to Eoin MacNeill, President of the Volunteer Corps, the IRB men were planning for a full-scale insurrection. They had formed a secret military council that included the tough old Fenian Tom Clarke and young Seán MacDermott, the IRB's national organiser. They were joined by Volunteers Patrick Pearse and Thomas MacDonagh, both of whom were academics, Eamonn Ceannt, a civil servant, and Joseph Mary Plunkett, whose father was a Director of the Museum of Science and Art.

Early in 1916 the military council committed to an armed uprising in the near future, and determined to persuade Connolly to join them. This time he was interested. He had begun a plan of action along similar lines. His Citizen Army was drilling with real firearms now, and in the basement of Liberty Hall he had a veritable munitions factory underway. At a private meeting with members of the military council – a meeting which may have been more like a kidnapping of Connolly – he agreed to join forces.

Some historians would later accuse Patrick Pearse of bloodthirstiness. Yet it was James Connolly who wrote, 'Deep in the heart of Ireland has sunk the sense of the degradation wrought upon its people, so deep and humiliating that no agency less powerful than the red tide of war on Irish soil will ever enable the

Irish race to recover its self-respect.'

The republicans had acquired a powerful and fearless ally.

On 18 April 1916, seven men signed the Proclamation of the Provisional Government of the Irish Republic, making insurrection fact. One of those seven was James Connolly. The signatories would form the core of the provisional government until public elections could be held. According to his wife, Tom Clarke was originally designated as President because he had been first to sign the Proclamation. However, the old Fenian, with years of secrecy behind him, preferred to work in the background. So that honour passed to Patrick Pearse, who had drafted the bulk of the Proclamation. Pearse was also appointed Commander-in-Chief, and James Connolly was named Commandant-General of the Dublin forces.

The rising was scheduled for Easter Sunday. But there was internal dissension. Eoin MacNeill, as the military council knew, was opposed to using the Volunteers for anything but defensive action. He countermanded the orders that had been issued, including those summoning thousands of Volunteers from the Irish countryside.

By this time the British authorities in Dublin Castle knew an insurrection was planned and were making plans of their own to arrest the ringleaders. If the rising did not go ahead at once, it never would. Pearse issued new orders for Easter Monday. On that day a vastly reduced force, including the Dublin Brigade of the Volunteers and the Irish Citizen Army, marched through Dublin and set up headquarters in the General Post Office on Sackville Street.

The week that followed was, perhaps, the most dramatic in Irish history. Outnumbered but never outfought, courageous in battle and gallant in defeat, the combined forces acquired a new name. James Connolly called them the Irish Republican Army (IRA).

When at last Pearse surrendered to prevent further bloodshed and save Dublin from being totally destroyed by British artillery, the men who had signed the Proclamation and led the Easter Rising were executed at Kilmainham Jail.

Connolly had been badly wounded during the fighting. In terrible pain from shattered bones and a gangrenous foot, he was among the last to die. Unable to stand, he faced the firing squad tied to a chair. But he did not flinch from death. James Connolly had never flinched from anything.

CHAPTER 12

Constance, Countess Markievicz (1868–1927)

'The Rebel Countess'

Constance Georgina Gore-Booth was born at Buckingham Gate, London. Her family were members of the Ascendancy, the landed Protestant class in Ireland. Among other properties, they owned Lissadell, an extensive estate in Sligo. Constance and her younger sister Eva Gore-Booth grew up in an atmosphere of wealth and privilege. William Butler Yeats was a frequent guest at their Sligo home, where he was inspired by the beauty of the two sisters to write one of his best-loved poems, 'Lissadell'. As a girl, Constance fell in love with the vision of Gaelic Ireland which Yeats's poetry evoked.

When she was of age, Constance was duly presented at court. Considered one of the beauties of her season, she could be expected to continue to lead the pampered life of a young woman of her class, revolving around dressmakers and travel, society soirées in London and Dublin, long weekends at country houses enlivened by shooting parties and hunt balls, and eventually a brilliant marriage. Her husband would be wealthy, preferably titled – and unquestionably Protestant. With all the conventions satisfied, Constance would then retire into dignified matronhood and raise another family of aristocrats.

Instead she went off on her own to London and Paris to study art. A photograph taken during that time shows her smoking a cigarette and wearing knickerbockers that revealed her lower legs. This was only a foretaste of things to come.

When she was 30 and a confirmed spinster living in Paris, Constance fell in love with Count Casimir Markievicz. He was not wealthy, being a second son, and his title was one of courtesy only. Worse yet, from the Ascendancy point of view, he was a Roman Catholic. 'Casi' was also six years younger than Constance and married, with two sons, though he was estranged from his wife. In 1899 Casi's wife died and Constance married him the next year.

Their only child, a daughter they named Maeve Alys, was born in 1901 at Lissadell. But Constance was neither wifely nor maternal by nature. Con, as her friends called her, showed a tendency to go her own way. Her husband referred to her as 'my loose cannon'. She had many enthusiasms and felt passionately about equality and women's suffrage. Invited to a meeting to discuss the establishment of a journal for women, she came straight from a dinner at Dublin Castle, still attired in her ball gown, and promptly offered to sell her jewellery to finance the project.

The women's movement in Ireland was not only supportive of suffrage, but nationalistic. Con joined the Sinn Féin party and further dismayed Ascendancy friends by becoming active in Inghínidhe na hÉireann and a regular contributor to the journal, *Bean na hÉireann*. Her Irish nationalism was becoming ever more apparent. In 1909 she helped to found Na Fianna Éireann, an organisation inspired by the boy scout movement in England. Con's Fianna were considerably more militant, however. A veteran of Big House shooting parties, Con taught them to shoot with a deadly accuracy they would put to good use later.

Convinced that her class had failed dismally in its duty to the underprivileged in Ireland, Constance Markievicz became an energetic activist for working-class causes. She set up free food kitchens, lectured Dublin's poor about nutrition and hygiene, and rescued children from the slums to incorporate into her Fianna. There she was able to see that they had good food to eat and decent uniforms to wear – mostly paid for out of her own funds. Eventually she would impoverish herself looking after others.

In 1910 King Edward VII died. Soon afterwards, at a theatrical performance attended by other members of the Ascendancy clad in mourning, Con appeared in a scarlet velvet gown. A soft-spoken woman, Con's actions shouted defiance, and such gestures made it obvious that she had broken with her class in order to champion a free Ireland.

When the new king, George V, undertook a state visit to Dublin, Sinn Féin formed a committee to organise opposition. Members of the Fianna were stationed along the route of the royal procession to distribute handbills inveighing against foreign rule. Con and Michael O'Rahilly spent hours stencilling a banner to be strung across Grafton Street, reading, 'Thou Art Not Conquered Yet, Dear Land'. During the procession Countess Markievicz was arrested for attempting to burn a Union Jack.

One of those in the crowd along the route was a young man called Eamon de Valera, who later remarked that this was the first time he had heard an Irish Republic advocated.

By this time an ardent socialist, Con was committed to the cause of Labour. During the Great Lock-Out in 1913 she was in the forefront of the crowd that gathered to hear Jim Larkin speak out against management. Larkin was wearing a coat borrowed from Con's husband when he was arrested. The riot that followed hardened positions on both sides. Dublin seethed with civil unrest. When James Connolly founded the Irish Citizen's Army to defend workers against police brutality, Countess Markievicz was one of its first recruits.

When the Irish National Volunteer Corps was formed as a counter to the Ulster Volunteer Force, Con joined Cumann na mBan, which was the female support group for the organisation. However, she resented the limitations placed upon Cumann na mBan by the male leadership of the Volunteers. She was able to be more physically active in the Citizen Army. James Connolly felt as she did about equality for women and made her an officer. Con took enthusiastic part in weapons practice and drilled in full uniform, though she did wear a skirt over her trousers.

The outbreak of the Great War saw the amicable demise of the Markievicz marriage. Count Casimir Markievicz went off to the Balkans as a war reporter and never lived in Dublin again.

During the Easter Rising of 1916 Countess Markievicz fought beside the men, serving as second-in-command to Michael Mallin in St Stephen's Green. She arrived at the Green in an open car accompanied by two members of the Fianna acting as her aides-de-camp. At once she set to work organising her troops. When actual battle broke out she was fearless under fire. Some witnesses claimed she killed at least one British soldier.

After the surrender Countess Markievicz refused a British officer's offer of motorised transport for herself, and marched away at the head of her company. She was tried for treason and sentenced to death. Her sentence was commuted, however – a concession to her sex that she bitterly resented. The male leaders of the rising were executed and she complained to friends that she had been discriminated against.

Con was imprisoned at Aylesbury in England until the general amnesty of 1917, then returned home to a hero's welcome and a torchlight parade through Dublin. Ireland adored its Rebel Countess. When Con converted to the Roman Catholic faith, her break from her Ascendancy background was complete.

The contempt the Irish felt for British government escalated after the rising. By 1918 another revolt seemed likely. Alarmed, in May the government used the excuse of an alleged 'German plot' to undertake wholesale arrests of nationalist leaders, including Con Markievicz. Her little dog, Poppet, was even arrested, obviously regarded as a dangerous German collaborator. Con was once more deported and this time imprisoned in Holloway Prison, London.

Whilst in prison, Con stood as a Sinn Féin candidate and became the first woman ever elected to the British parliament. In accordance with Sinn Féin policy she refused to take her seat. Instead, upon her release in 1919 she became a member of the first Dáil Éireann and was appointed Minister for Labour. During the War of Independence ministers for the Irish Republic were on the run and Con was no exception. She served two more jail sentences, one in Cork and one in Mountjoy Jail in Dublin.

Con vehemently opposed the Treaty of 1921 and the partitioning of Ireland. Speaking of the Treaty, she said, 'While Ireland is not free I remain a rebel, unconverted and inconvertible.' The following year she toured America to rally support for the republican cause.

Arrested yet again in 1923, Con went on hunger strike. When Eamon de Valera founded the republican Fianna Fáil party in 1926 she joined immediately, and was re-elected to the Dáil in 1927. By this time her health was failing, however. Casi came back to Ireland to be with her at the end. Ireland's indomitable Rebel Countess died on 15 July 1927, and was buried in Glasnevin Cemetery in Dublin.

CHAPTER 13

James Larkin (1876–1947)

'Big Jim'

James Larkin was the second son of Jim and Mary Larkin, Irish immigrants from Ulster who settled in Liverpool. Liverpool is generally given as James Larkin's birthplace. According to family records, however, he may have been born in County Down, when his mother travelled home to see her dying father. During his trial in New York in 1920 he gave his birthplace as Tamnaharry, near Newry, County Down.

In his early childhood Larkin was cared for in Ireland by his widowed grandmother, Cathy McAnulty. His mother returned to her husband in Liverpool and bore four more children, the last of whom died at birth. At the age of nine young James Larkin sought employment on the Liverpool docks. His first wage was half a crown – 12½ pence – a week. When their father died prematurely, James and his older brother, Hugh, were under intense financial pressure to help support the family. James stowed away on a ship bound for Montevideo in South America. In a precursor to his life's work, he organised other stowaways on board to obtain better food and conditions.

James, now known as Jim, returned to Liverpool in 1894. Hugh had emigrated to America by that time, and Jim and his younger brother, Peter, worked on the docks. During this time Jim had an accident and was laid off for many months, during which time he undertook the self-education that would stand him in good stead for the rest of his life. He also became interested in socialism and trade unionism, joining the National Union of Dock Labourers in 1901.

In 1903 Jim Larkin married Elizabeth Brown, the daughter of a Baptist lay preacher who managed a temperance café. Their courtship consisted of his taking her to trade union and socialist meetings, which must have been something of a shock to a gentle young woman raised in an atmosphere of religious evangelism. The marriage, though one of chalk and cheese, was a loving one. Elizabeth bore Jim four sons: Jim Junior, Denis, Finton and Barney.

In 1907 James Sexton, who was the leader of the union, recognised the passion in Larkin. He made him a union organiser and sent him to Belfast. Larkin was thrown into the deep end amongst bitter, dispirited men who were divided by rampant sectarianism. A lesser individual might have thought the situation hopeless; Larkin set about establishing a strong branch of the union. He drew attention like a lightning rod. A towering figure, electric with vitality and possessed of a gift for mesmerising oratory, he made speeches throughout the Belfast dock area as well as in the heart of the city. Soon the workers were flocking to him.

Predictably, the employers who had been successfully exploiting cheap Belfast labour for years set out to break the new union. Members were locked out, which prompted a strike by the city's dockers and carters that lasted from May through November of 1907. Many factories were closed, a crippling blow for the industrial capital of Ireland. Police protection had to be called in for those who attempted to cross the picket lines. But the sympathies of the police, who were also stirred by Larkin's fiery eloquence, were with the strikers. Three hundred members of the Royal Irish Constabulary mutinied on behalf of Larkin and his followers.

While the Independent Orange Order, a Protestant organisation, officially supported Larkin, behind the scenes there was a campaign of sectarianism that attempted to divide the workers once more. Rioting broke out and two men were shot dead by troops on the Falls Road. The union was providing strike pay for the workers, but as the situation continued James Sexton became concerned that the cost would bankrupt the parent union. Going over Larkin's head, he arranged a settlement directly with the employers which Larkin saw as surrender.

Jim Larkin felt betrayed by the English-based union. This only served to strengthen his growing sense of the importance of Irish nationalism. He broke his ties with Sexton's organisation and in 1909 founded the Irish Transport and General Workers' Union (ITGWU). Its membership included tram drivers, carters, dockers, labourers and factory workers, a broad spectrum of Dublin's most impoverished citizenry, at a time when the Dublin slums were among the worst in Europe.

With a unique combination of socialism, trade unionism and Irish nationalism, Larkin developed a following in the tens of thousands. Dublin employers were as alarmed by his magnetic leadership as Belfast employers had been. They banded into a federation led by William Martin Murphy, the owner of the *Irish Independent* newspaper and director of the Dublin United Tramways Company. Murphy, who hated the very idea of trade unions, set out to break Larkin. In 1913 he demanded that all those who worked for him, either on the newspaper or the trams, must leave the ITGWU. When the workers refused, he locked them out.

Other unions supported their fellow workers. The other members of the Employers' Federation followed Murphy's example, and so began the Great Lock-Out. It was to last for eight months and would be characterised by repeated police brutality. At least 100,000 people would be thrown out of work before it was over. The workers kept up one another's spirits by sharing what little they had, even when they were reduced to near-starvation. Food shipments were sent from fellow trade unionists in England, although English unions did not support the Irish with a sympathetic strike.

Big Jim Larkin, the first man to challenge authority on their behalf, had become a hero to Dublin's working poor. The government charged him with seditious conspiracy. He managed to evade arrest until the day he appeared, heavily disguised, at a proscribed union rally in Sackville Street. It was the last Sunday in August 1913, and Dublin's great boulevard was crowded with pedestrians returning from Mass. Police swooped down with batons and sabres to sieze Larkin, and a riot ensued. One man and a woman were killed outright, while a second man died the next day. Scores were badly injured, flooding city hospitals.

Jim Larkin was sentenced to seven months in prison. The authorities also demanded that the national schools refuse to educate 'the children of the criminal Larkin'. Had it not been for a headmaster called Patrick Pearse, who defied the government and took Larkin's sons into Saint Enda's, they would have received no schooling.

Throughout this time Jim Larkin's strongest ally was union organiser James Connolly, who eventually obtained Larkin's release by using the union to close Dublin port. With imports shut off and business crippled, the government capitulated to the extent of freeing Big Jim. The Great Lock-Out ended with no clear victory for either side, but the workers had established certain rights that they would never relinquish, and had taught their employers a new respect for the power of the unions.

However, the ITGWU had exhausted itself in trying to maintain the striking workers and their families. Leaving Connolly in charge, in 1914 Larkin went off to America to raise funds. To his dismay he found American employers to be even more antagonistic to the concept of the trade union than those in Europe. Larkin was deeply touched by the plight of the American workers. He went to work on their behalf as passionately and tirelessly as he had done in Ireland, devoting all of his energies to their cause. Once again he clashed with the might of capitalism, this time in an economy where the employers had tremendous power. Eventually, in 1920, Jim Larkin was arrested and charged with criminal anarchy. His sentence was five to ten years indeterminate imprisonment in New York's Sing Sing Prison.

While in prison Larkin received many visitors, not only labour leaders and trade unionists, but celebrities such as Paul Robeson, Charlie Chaplin and actress Merle Oberon. Michael Collins smuggled Jim Larkin Junior and Thomas Foran, the President of the ITGWU, to America to see him. Jim Junior remained there for six months, a great comfort to his father. Supporters bombarded politicians with pleas for the release of the man who had 'gone to prison for loyalty to the working class'. After three years Larkin was pardoned by New York Governor Al Smith, and it was strongly suggested to him that he return to Ireland.

Shortly after his arrival in Ireland he spent a few weeks recuperating from his ordeal at Lissadell, the family estate of his great friend and supporter, Countess Markievicz. She was one of the few who remained loyal to him from the old days. During Big Jim's imprisonment in America it had become obvious that he and his wife had grown apart, and although they held one another in great affection for the rest of their lives, they would never live together again.

The Ireland to which Larkin had returned was a land forever changed by the 1916 Rising. James Connolly was dead and the ITGWU had developed along new lines. The executive committee viewed Larkin's arrival with some apprehension, fearing there was likely to be disagreement with the man they called 'the stormy petrel' of the union. They were right. Larkin felt they were not adhering sufficiently to the principles of socialism. A dispute arose that led to his expulsion.

Together with his brother Peter, Jim Larkin founded a new organisation called the Workers' Union of Ireland (WUI). The WUI harkened back to the early principles of Larkinism. Jim entered the political arena as a Dublin city councillor, and also served three terms as a deputy in Dáil Éireann, from 1927–1932, from 1937–1938 and from 1943–1944. He remained a man of deep conviction and unflagging generosity.

During the early forties he continued to campaign tirelessly on behalf of workers' rights. His last major achievement was to secure a fortnight's annual leave for manual workers – a concession which took a 14-week strike to win. To the end he lived simply and honestly, a man who always put the needs of others above his own. When Larkin died on 30 January 1947, he left £4.6s0 and a few personal belongings. He is buried in Glasnevin Cemetery in Dublin.

Big Jim Larkin is remembered and much loved in Dublin even today, not as a fighter in the cause of national freedom, but as a fighter in the cause of human dignity. That is his legacy.

CHAPTER 14

Patrick Henry Pearse (1879–1916)

'The Pure Flame'

In the west wing of Dublin's Kilmainham Jail a gloomy passageway is lined on either side with tiny cells. While the rest of the prison has been brightly refurbished and now welcomes visitors, this dark heart of Kilmainham remains as it was in 1916. From these lightless cells the leaders of the Easter Rising went forth to meet the firing squad. And here, on the night before his death, Patrick Pearse wrote a poem called 'The Wayfarer':

Sometimes my heart hath shaken with great joy,
To see a leaping squirrel in a tree,
Or a red lady-bird upon a stalk,
Or little rabbits in a field at evening,
Lit by a slanting sun.

Patrick Henry Pearse, who bore the same names as the American patriot who said, 'Give me liberty or give me death,' was born in Dublin. His father James, an Englishman, had come to Ireland in his youth with a group of ecclesiastical craftsmen. In time he was able to open his own business and gained eminence as a sculptor of monumental stone figures. Many of Dublin's churches and public buildings were adorned with his work.

James Pearse was a middle-aged widower with two grown children when he met and married an Irish Catholic girl called Margaret Brady. The couple settled at 27 Great Brunswick Street – now Pearse Street. Although of Protestant stock, by the time of Patrick's birth James Pearse had converted to Catholicism.

Patrick was the oldest of four children, having a younger brother, William, and two sisters, Margaret and Mary Brigid. They were a close-knit and loving family, but Willie in particular idolised Patrick. His was a devotion that would last to the grave.

Patrick Pearse received the best education his parents could provide. The Christian Brothers' school he attended introduced him to the Irish language. Meanwhile an elderly relative of his mother's lit an early flame of patriotism in the boy with old tales of hardship and heroism. He set about learning all he could of Ireland's history and teaching himself more of the Irish language.

Pearse was not the only person bent on re-discovering past glories. A Celtic Renaissance was underway, spearheaded by the Gaelic League. The League had been founded in 1893 by renowned Irish scholar Douglas Hyde and Professor Eoin MacNeill among others. When Pearse joined the organisation in 1896 it was non-political, dedicated only to preserving, restoring and spreading the Irish language and culture.

Pearse, who at 17 was an ardent Gaelic nationalist of the mystical rather than revolutionary sort, threw himself wholeheartedly into work for the League. He was soon co-opted onto the executive committee and began signing his name in Irish, Pádraic mac Piarais. That same year Pearse founded the New Ireland Literary Society, whose aim was to popularise Irish poetry and folklore amongst those to whom it was unfamiliar.

In 1898 Pearse entered the Royal University. He was a highly intelligent man who preferred reading to athletics and strove to excel at everything he did. His future looked bright. The family was accustomed to a nice home and a comfortable standard of living, but this was disrupted by the death of James Pearse in 1900. Most of James's estate was tied up in his business. Patrick was still studying for his degree and Willie, at 18, was finishing his third year in art school. Neither was equipped to take over the family business but they did, agreeing to run it together as best they could. They moved into a smaller house and Patrick Pearse began what would be a lifelong struggle to provide for his widowed mother and siblings.

In spite of this burden he managed to take a BA degree in law and was called to the bar in 1901. Like many another idealistic young lawyer he believed he would be championing justice. In 1905 he defended a Donegal farmer whose only crime was painting his name in Irish on his cart, for which he was given a fine he could not pay. Pearse's pleading on his behalf was described by the judge as 'ingenious, interesting, and from a literary point of view, instructive'. However, the court found against his client.

Pearse thereupon gave up the practice of law, which he would later describe as 'the most ignoble of all professions'. Instead he entered the field of education, hoping to pass the pure flame of his great love for Ireland on to a new generation.

From 1903 to 1909 Pearse edited the Gaelic League periodical, *An Claidheamh Soluis*. During this time he wrote a number of plays, poems and short stories, touchingly innocent and Gaelic in tone, while his more serious writings reflected the increasingly overt nationalism of both the League and himself.

In his late twenties he was romantically attracted to Eibhlín Nichols, a UCD graduate and as ardent a patriot as Pearse. Letters indicate that she returned his affection, but tragically she died in a drowning accident off the Blasket Islands while saving another girl. A grief-stricken Pearse attended her funeral.

Thereafter Patrick Pearse invested his capacity for devotion in Ireland's future, specifically the children. In 1908 he founded Saint Enda's College, a secondary school for boys in Cullenswood House in Rathmines, Dublin. By 1910 the school had outgrown its quarters and moved to a leased country estate known as the Hermitage in Rathfarnham. Cullenswood House was converted into Saint Ita's, a school for girls.

Pearse proved to be an educational revolutionary. The official school language was Irish. To prepare students for life in a bilingual society, all subjects except English, French and the sciences were taught in both English and Irish. Nature study and self-reliance were high on the agenda, ranking with the study of the classics. Great emphasis was placed on personal honour, moral values and most of all on patriotism.

Pearse was determined that his students should be sound in body as well as mind. Classes were taught outdoors when the weather allowed and instruction was given in all forms of sport, particularly Gaelic games. The production of musicals and theatrical performances helped raise funds for the school, which was always struggling financially in spite of support by family friends and members of the Gaelic League. Some of the Saint Enda's boys appeared at the Abbey Theatre in plays written by Pearse himself.

Pearse also published numerous essays on his educational theories. His best-known, 'The Murder Machine', condemned the existing British system of schooling as crippling to the young mind. His writings were attracting considerable attention for their defiantly nationalistic tone when, in 1913, Patrick Pearse joined the Irish Republican Brotherhood (IRB).

Also in 1913, Sir Edward Carson founded a new Ulster Volunteer Force (UVF) with the tacit compliance of the British government. As a counter to the UVF, in 1914 the Irish National Volunteer Corps was founded by Eoin MacNeill and others. MacNeill was elected President. One of the members of the Provisional Committee was Patrick Pearse, who was later named Organising Director. Pearse was assigned to Rathfarnham E Company, 4th Battalion, Dublin Brigade. For weaponry to use in drilling the Brigade relied initially on oak batons like those carried by the police, which was a relief to Pearse, who had never fired a gun in his life and loathed violence.

But violence was coming ever closer. Unbeknown to Eoin MacNeill, the Volunteers were infiltrated by the IRB – of which Patrick Pearse was also a member. The Brotherhood had long been convinced of the need to use physical force if Ireland was ever to throw off British rule.

In September of 1915 Patrick Pearse was promoted to the Supreme Council of the IRB. He, Joseph Plunkett and Eamonn Ceannt formed an advisory committee to draw up military plans for an insurrection. None of the three had any military background. What they did have was a thorough knowledge of the Dublin area and an understanding of the forces arranged against them. The undertaking was not hopeless, although some historians would later try to claim it was. Distracted by the war in Europe, the British had drastically reduced the number of troops stationed in Ireland in order to send more men to the trenches. Throughout the country there were over 100,000 Volunteers. They had acquired some weapons through the offices of the IRB and were anticipating many more. Even ill-trained and ill-equipped, they were fired with patriotism and eager to fight for Ireland's freedom.

Based on these factors, Pearse and the military council of the IRB believed the rising might succeed where so many had failed. Surely there would never be a better time to strike for independence.

In the weeks and months that followed there was a flurry of preparatory activity. Sir Roger Casement, an Irish-born former British consul celebrated as 'the Hero of the Congo', hoped to persuade the Germans to supply arms and support Ireland's struggle against Britain. Troop drills were stepped up and an effort undertaken to win James Connolly and his Citizen Army to the cause.

A document was drafted, primarily by Pearse, and prepared for distribution when the time came. The Proclamation of the Irish Republic would make fact of a long-cherished dream. It was signed by seven men who thereby took on the duties of forming a provisional government: Thomas J Clarke, Seán Mac Diarmada, PH Pearse, James Connolly, Thomas MacDonagh, Eamonn Ceannt and Joseph Plunkett.

The date for the uprising was fixed as Easter Sunday, 1916 – when the British would least expect it. The usual exodus from Dublin would mean that many officials and bureaucrats were away for the holidays. Patrick Pearse, as Commander-in Chief, issued the final orders, but MacNeill – who passionately believed in using the Volunteers for defensive purposes only – furiously countermanded them.

By that time Dublin Castle had learned from an informer of the plans for an uprising and was preparing to arrest the suspected leaders. If the rising did not go ahead, within days they would all be in prison and the chance would be lost forever. So Pearse issued a new set of orders – for Easter Monday.

There was not enough time to re-group. Messages failed to get through. Many of the Volunteers in rural areas, believing the rising was called off, had gone away for Easter. The number that answered Pearse's call on Monday was minute compared with the number originally anticipated. It is estimated that less than 2000 altogether – including the Citizen Army and members of the Fianna – gathered to challenge the armed might of the British Empire.

As they marched away from Liberty Hall that morning their leaders knew a military victory was no longer possible. The best they could do was acquit themselves nobly and pray that their actions would be enough to encourage the Irish people to shake off years of apathy and subservience.

Patrick Pearse spent Easter Week in the General Post Office on Sackville Street (now O'Connell Street), headquarters for the republican forces. From beneath its portico he read the Proclamation of the Republic to a largely uninterested citizenry. In a belt at his waist he carried a Browning automatic pistol which was never fired. He took no part in the fighting; instead he spent considerable time writing optimistic newsletters to cheer the populace. By the end of the week, when the GPO was ablaze, he finally ordered evacuation of the building. On 29 April he surrendered, in order to spare Dublin further destruction and bloodshed.

The republicans were arrested and taken to jail. At Pearse's order they behaved themselves in strict accordance with the conventions of war. Their weapons were handed over without argument; some men even went home to wash and change their clothes before turning themselves in.

Their leaders were court-martialled and secretly executed a few at a time, to drag out the punishment. Patrick Pearse spent his last night writing in his cell. In his farewell letter to his mother he told her, 'This is the death I should have asked for if God had given me the choice of all deaths.' Then he penned 'The Wayfarer', summing up his love of the life he was so soon to leave.

At 3:30am on 3 May, Patrick Pearse was marched to the Stonebreakers' Yard in Kilmainham Jail and shot dead by a firing squad. His body was not returned to his mother. Instead he and the other members of the Provisional Government of the Irish Republic, as well as Willie Pearse, whose greatest crime was that of following where his brother led, were buried in quicklime in unmarked graves at Kilmainham and at Arbour Hill Prison.

CHAPTER 15

Terence MacSwiney, Lord Mayor of Cork (1879–1920)

'Rebel Lord Mayor'

Like a number of other Irish patriots, Terence MacSwiney grew up without a father during his formative years. And like at least one other, Patrick Pearse, he had an English-born parent.

Terence MacSwiney was the son of a restless Cork man, John MacSwiney, and an Englishwoman, Mary Wilkinson, who met and married while John was a school-teacher in London. They had three young children when John decided to take his family to Ireland and open a tobacco factory in Cork City. In Cork the MacSwineys had six more children, including Terence. Unfortunately the tobacco business went bankrupt and the family was left almost destitute.

In 1885 John MacSwiney again succumbed to the urge to change his life. He emigrated to Australia and subsequently died in Melbourne, leaving his wife in Ireland to raise their children by herself. She was a devout Catholic who inculcated her children with her own deep faith and spiritual values.

As a child Terence MacSwiney, whom everyone called 'Terry', was bright, talkative and full of mischief. He also proved to be an excellent scholar. After completing his secondary education at the

Christian Brothers' school at North Monastery in Cork City, he went to work as an entry level clerk at Dwyer and Co., a Cork warehousing and distribution company. He was only 15 years old.

The idea of emigrating appealed to him as it had to his father, but he was now helping to support the family. He would always retain a strong sense of responsibility. He was close to all his family, but particularly to his sister Mary, who was eight years older than himself. She would remain important to him throughout his life.

MacSwiney dreamed of attending university and studying medicine, until a breakdown of his health due to overwork prevented his undertaking the entrance exam. His real passion was the Irish separatist cause, however. Cork was strongly nationalistic and both Terence and his sister, Mary, absorbed this influence from early childhood.

In 1899 MacSwiney and some friends formed the Cork Celtic Literary Society. The society soon involved itself in political activities, including a dramatic public protest at the visit of King Edward VII to the Cork Exhibition in 1902. This occasioned the first, though not the last, arrest of Terence MacSwiney.

Although he had always loved to write, about this time he developed an interest in journalism and began contributing to such periodicals as the Dublin-based *Irish Freedom*. His patriotic essays reflect the passionate, romantic fervour of the period – the love of Ireland that was coming powerfully to the fore among a new generation.

In 1904 MacSwiney's mother died and his sister, Mary, took over her duties as the focus of the household. She encouraged her brother in his literary interests, and also in furthering his education, while he continued to work in the accounting department of

Dwyer and Co. In 1907 MacSwiney graduated from the Royal University of Cork with a degree in Mental and Moral Science.

In 1908, with Daniel Corkery, he founded the Cork Dramatic Society. Several of the plays he wrote were performed by the society.

The field of teaching attracted him, and he obtained an appointment to work part-time as a lecturer in business methods at the Cork Municipal School of Commerce. The following year MacSwiney applied for the post of commercial teacher and organiser of classes in the towns of County Cork – a full-time position. His employers and co-workers at Dwyer and Co. provided him with glowing recommendations and he was accepted.

His work travelling around the county provided him with the background and contacts he would use in helping to form the Cork Volunteers in 1913. In 1914 MacSwiney wrote and published a weekly paper called *Fianna Fáil*, which focused on the republican movement and was suppressed by the government after only 11 issues. He continued to write for other nationalist papers, however, in addition to becoming, in 1915, a full-time organiser for the Irish Volunteers with the rank of Commandant.

At Christmas in 1915, Terence MacSwiney attended a musical evening with a friend. There he met Muriel Murphy, the daughter of one of Cork's most prominent families, owners of the distillery that still produces Paddy's Whiskey and Murphy's Stout. The Murphys were among Cork's wealthiest Catholics.

From their first meeting Muriel was impressed by the handsome, intense young man. When MacSwiney was arrested in January of 1916 for making a seditious speech, her interest was, if anything, piqued. She knew no republicans, and certainly no one like Terry. MacSwiney was released in February without being brought to trial and their courtship began in earnest – despite the strong opposition of her family. The Murphys were described as being 'very Anglo', an attitude which may have been necessary to maintain their position in Cork City, dominated as it was by an English garrison. The last thing they wanted was for Muriel to marry an Irish rebel.

Muriel, however, was rebellious herself. Disregarding her family, she undertook the study of Irish to please Terry. During his periods in jail, which were becoming more frequent as the government attempted to quash the republican movement, the two exchanged frequent impassioned letters.

On Easter Sunday, 1916, Terence MacSwiney received a copy of Eoin MacNeill's orders countermanding the original plan for the Easter Rising. He obeyed as a good soldier should. The failure of himself and the other Cork Volunteers to take part in the rebellion would haunt MacSwiney for the rest of his life.

In June 1917, Terence MacSwiney and Muriel Murphy were married – although the groom was in prison at the time. Richard Mulcahy, who would become Chief-of-Staff of the Irish Republican Army, served as the best man. On their wedding day MacSwiney wrote a letter to Muriel's mother from his prison cell, assuring her that he meant to take the best possible care of her daughter.

Upon his release from prison MacSwiney and Muriel set up house in Douglas Road in Cork City. They had three extremely happy months before he was arrested yet again. In all, he would be jailed six times between 1916 and 1920. He saw his baby daughter Máire for the first time when Muriel went to visit him in prison in Belfast.

Meanwhile, survivors of the Easter Rising such as Eamon de Valera, Michael Collins and Cathal Brugha, together with prominent republicans such as Arthur Griffith and Count Joseph Plunkett, were dedicated to establishing the Irish Republic that Patrick Pearse had proclaimed. In the general election of 1918, the Sinn Féin political party founded by Griffith promised Irish voters that if their candidates were elected, they would not take their seats in the British parliament. Instead they would establish an Irish national assembly.

The Irish people, by an overwhelming majority, voted Sinn Féin into office. Out of 105 members elected to parliament, 73 were Republicans, six belonged to the Irish Parliamentary Party, which was also nationalist. The Unionists retained but 26 seats, having polled a majority in only four of the nine northern counties. In all of Ireland, out of a total of 1,525,910 votes registered, the Unionists (official and independent combined) received only 315,394 – about one-fifth. The people of Ireland had voted for the Republic and Irish independence.

On 21 January 1919, Dáil Éireann – the Assembly of Ireland – met in inaugural session. The British refused to recognise the new government or the right of the Irish people to govern themselves. They proscribed the organisation and began a series of raids and arrests, which only served to drive the members underground. But the rebels would not give up their dream of a Republic. To that end they began putting in place the necessary mechanisms for governing a nation.

Terence MacSwiney was elected to the Dáil in 1919. He served on the Foreign Affairs Committee and was active in matters relating to trade and commerce. His business acumen was invaluable to Michael Collins, who put him in charge of fundraising for the new government in Cork.

Meanwhile, MacSwiney continued to serve as Second-in-Command of the Cork Brigade of the Irish Republican Army, under his friend, Commandant Tomás MacCurtáin. MacCurtáin was also Lord Mayor of Cork – until he was assassinated by forces of the Crown on 18 March 1920.

On 30 March, Terence MacSwiney was elected Lord Mayor of Cork. Refusing to be intimidated by the fate of his predecessor, he announced, 'Our first duty is to answer the threat in the only fitting manner by showing ourselves unterrified, cool, and inflexible for the fulfilment of our purpose – the establishment of the independence and integrity of our country … we ask for no mercy and we will make no compromise.'

Prophetic words in light of what was to come.

A new military force had been created by the British government in an effort to break the spirit of the nationalists: a combination of a volunteer police force and Cadet Auxiliaries, known locally as the Black and Tans. They ran amok in the countryside, acting outside of military control. Violence escalated by the day as hundreds of people were shot, flogged or burned out of their homes. Dublin Castle, seat of the British bureaucracy in Ireland, claimed that the victims of the Black and Tans were being murdered by 'republican extremists'.

They had made the same claim for the death of Tomás MacCurtáin. However, a coroner's jury found that MacCurtáin's murder had taken place 'under circumstances of most callous brutality', and was 'organised and carried out by the Royal Irish

Constabulary officially directed by the British government'. The new Lord Mayor of Cork made certain that these findings were made public.

On 12 August, British soldiers raided City Hall. They arrested Terence MacSwiney, together with several ranking Irish Volunteers whom the arresting officers failed to recognise. MacSwiney proposed that they immediately go on hunger strike to protest what he considered an illegal action by a foreign government in the Republic of Ireland. After three days the other Volunteers were released, but MacSwiney was bound over for a court martial. He was charged with having British secret codes in his possession.

Although the circumstances of the arrest and the evidence brought against the Lord Mayor were highly questionable, on 16 August MacSwiney was convicted and sentenced to two years' hard labour.

After the sentence was read out, Terence MacSwiney rose to make the statement allowed him under the law. He informed the court that he had taken no food since his arrest, and said, 'I will put a limit to any term of imprisonment you may impose. I have decided the terms of my detention whatever your government may do. I shall be free, alive or dead, within a month.'

He was transported to Brixton Prison in London, England. By the time he arrived he had grown so weak that the prison doctor decided against any effort to force-feed him. Meanwhile MacSwiney's situation was attracting international attention. What might be done with impunity to unknown men and women could not so easily be done to the elected Lord Mayor of a large city.

Newspapers as far away as the United States soon were reporting, 'The Lord Mayor is not expected to live more than a few hours.' They reckoned without the unshakeable resolve of the man. MacSwiney wanted to stay alive as long as possible, not only in the hope that the British government might back down, but also to draw world attention to the Irish cause.

His agony was acute.

As the hunger strike continued the British government was besieged by letters from prominent personages, urging clemency. Foreign journalists were arriving by the score. One, a Frenchman, wrote, 'Two wills confront each other. One is in a prison. The other is in a palace. Which will be the stronger?' The German press predicted, 'If MacSwiney dies ... if he diverts all arrows of racial hatred to his own heart ... the Lord Mayor of Cork will be more powerful in his death than the Prime Minister or the King of England.'

Having survived without food for an incredible 74 days, Terence MacSwiney, Lord Mayor of Cork, died at Brixton Prison on 24 October 1920.

Chapter 16

Michael Collins (1890–1922)

'The Big Fellow'

Michael John Collins was 75 years old when his last child was born on a farm near Clonakilty, County Cork. In his sixtieth year Michael John had married a 23-year-old local girl called Marianne O'Brien. He was an extraordinarily vigorous man, of whom one of his daughters wrote, 'My father never had an old age.' Marianne bore him eight children. The son they named Michael was the last, and would become a legend in his own lifetime.

His father, who had educated himself to a high standard, died when the boy was seven. On his deathbed Michael Collins Senior predicted of his last-born, 'One day he'll be a great man. He'll do great work for Ireland.' Such a prophecy, coming from the seventh son of a seventh son, was not taken lightly.

The Collins's farm, Woodfield, consisted of 90 acres. With eight children to help with the work the place was almost self-sufficient, so that even without a father the Collins family was relatively affluent by local standards. Michael Collins was educated under the national school system which taught pupils to say, 'Thank God I am a happy English child'! There was a strong streak of the rebel in the Collins children, however. Michael's sister, Marianne, once infuriated her teachers by proclaiming in front of visiting dignitaries, 'Thank God I am a happy Irish child!'

As he grew, Michael Collins was thoroughly inculcated with the history of his native country. A schoolmaster, Denis Lyons, was an active member of the Irish Republican Brotherhood and taught young Michael about Wolfe Tone and revolution together with reading, writing and arithmetic. The life he saw around him had a profound effect on the boy. Speaking of a local landlord with a reputation for brutally evicting his tenants, Collins told a cousin, 'When I'm a man we'll have him and his kind out of Ireland.'

As soon as he was old enough, Collins took the examinations necessary for joining the Civil Service. In 1906, at the age of 16, he was hired as a postal clerk and sent to London. There he studied Irish in classes run by the Gaelic League – and also joined Sinn Féin. From the post office he went on to work for a firm of stockbrokers, adding a knowledge of financial matters to his understanding of the British bureaucracy. By 1909 he had become a member of the Irish Republican Brotherhood. In 1914 he and a number of other expatriates joined a company of Irish Volunteers rather than enlist in the British army.

Early in 1916 Michael Collins returned to Dublin to take part in the Easter Rising. He served as aide-de-camp to Joseph Mary Plunkett in the General Post Office. Arrested with the other Irish Volunteers after the surrender, Collins was imprisoned at Frongoch Internment Camp in Wales. Frongoch became notorious as a 'university for revolutionaries', and it was there that Collins's talent for leadership came to the fore.

Upon being released in the Christmas amnesty of 1916, Collins returned to Dublin and immediately went to work for republican causes. He took a job as secretary to the Irish National Aid Fund, established by Tom Clarke's widow to help the dependants of dead or imprisoned Volunteers. Elected to the Sinn Féin executive committee, he began a meteoric rise through the republican political structure. In October 1917 Collins was appointed Director of Organisation for the reactivated Irish Volunteers, by then known as the Irish Republican Army (IRA). He also became a member of the Supreme Council of the Irish Republican Brotherhood (IRB).

Collins began recruiting men to form an intelligence squad to counter the British intelligence service. Early recruits included members of G Division, the political detective wing in Dublin Castle. By having in his service the very men who were being paid to spy on the republicans, Collins gained access to the government's most sensitive material.

In the 1918 general election the Sinn Féin Party won a large number of seats by promising to continue the struggle for Irish independence. Dáil Éireann, the national assembly democratically elected to replace British government in Ireland, was established by Sinn Féin. Michael Collins was appointed Minister for Home Affairs and subsequently Minister for Finance, responsible for raising funds in Ireland and abroad. He was so successful at this that the Dáil Loan – the bond issue that was to fund the new government – was heavily oversubscribed.

But Collins's real enthusiasm was for intelligence work. Like his father, he was a man of astonishing energy. His nature was a mass of contradictions. Painstaking and methodical about details, he could be incredibly reckless with his own safety. He often wheeled around Dublin on his bicycle with top-secret documents concealed in his socks.

The British were increasingly aware of Collins's activities, but were unable to catch him. They could not even identify him. Collins was on good terms with the police and fostered many contacts outside Dublin Castle. Nicknamed 'the Big Fellow', he was both a man's man and a woman's man. Handsome, athletic and gregarious, he won the admiration of his comrades-in-arms and the devotion of a number of sweethearts.

British resistance to Ireland's continuing demands for freedom from foreign domination increased. The Dáil was forced underground by constant raids and arrests. More of its members were in prison than out at any given time. Still it struggled to put in place the structures that would govern a fledgling republic.

March 1920 saw the arrival of a British quasi-police force, the Black and Tans. They operated outside of military control and had only one brief: to destroy Irish nationalism. The reign of violence they initiated signalled the start of a struggle the British would call the Anglo-Irish War. To Irish nationalists it was, at first, the Tan War – and then the War of Independence. This time they were resolved to fight all the way to freedom.

Michael Collins would prove to be a decisive factor in the War of Independence. He seemed to be everywhere at once, elusive as the Scarlet Pimpernel, as he crippled the British intelligence system. Without their network of spies and paid informers, the authorities were unable to maintain control over the country. Irish Volunteers in Cork and Limerick, Kerry and Clare, in Waterford, Wexford and Tipperary, battered British forces. Tax records were burnt. Local government ground to a halt. Much of the judicial system, which had been heavily weighted on the side of the ruling class, was supplanted by Sinn Féin courts of arbitration.

As the War of Independence continued, British losses mounted. Military advisors warned the Prime Minister, Lloyd George, that His Majesty's forces were so demoralised they would soon have to be withdrawn from Ireland and totally replaced. The death on hunger strike of the Lord Mayor of Cork, Terence MacSwiney, further turned international opinion against the policy Lloyd George's Conservative/Liberal coalition government was pursuing in Ireland.

In the summer of 1921 Lloyd George made overtures of peace to Eamon de Valera, the president of Dáil Éireann. Negotiations between the two were difficult, but eventually a truce was agreed upon to give time to work out a settlement. The Irish were optimistic that Lloyd George would at last recognise the Irish Republic. Michael Collins, with few men and minuscule resources compared to the might of the British Empire, had at last forced the British to the negotiating table.

The Treaty Delegation led by Collins and Arthur Griffith, the founder of Sinn Féin, went to London in the winter of 1921. Eamon de Valera chose not to attend. The negotiations that followed were protracted and agonising. Lloyd George was determined that Ireland should not become an independent republic. This would signal a diminution of an Empire already in danger of being whittled away by the demands of nationalists in India, Egypt and elsewhere.

Conservatives on the British negotiating team, such as Winston Churchill, were equally determined to partition Ireland in order to placate the Unionists in the northeast of the country. The Unionist vote in parliament was essential to the Conservative Party if it wanted to remain in government.

Negotiations dragged on over several wearying weeks. Haggling over petty details, arguments about the interpretation of obscure wording, constant political posturing, confrontation and obfuscation wore down the Irish delegation. For the most part men of action, they were not prepared for the political manipulation at which Lloyd George and his team were so adept.

When the Irish were at the end of their tether both physically and psychologically, Lloyd George warned them that if they did not sign at once, war would break out within three days. Winston Churchill said afterward,

'Michael Collins rose looking as if he was going to shoot someone, preferably himself. In all my life, I have never seen so much passion and suffering in restraint.'

The Anglo–Irish Treaty was signed on 6 December 1921. Under this treaty, 26 counties of Ireland would become the Irish Free State, similar to the Dominion status granted to Canada, New Zealand, Australia and South Africa. The Free State would also allow Britain free use of its harbours and other facilities, which amounted to agreeing to continued occupation. Members of the parliament of the Free State would also take an oath of fidelity to the British sovereign.

The price of this limited independence was the dismemberment of Ireland. Six northeastern counties would remain within the Union, forming an artificial statelet called Northern Ireland.

The exhausted Treaty delegation returned to Ireland convinced they had done their best under the circumstances, but aware that there would be an enormous backlash from those who had fought so long and hard for a republic. Michael Collins said, quite bluntly, that in signing the Treaty he had signed his own death warrant.

The conflict over the Treaty, both inside the Dáil and throughout the country, was bitterly divisive. Constance Markievicz, for example, was scathing in her denunciation of the agreement. Its supporters pointed out that it gained more from the British than Ireland had ever had before. Opponents were adamant that the negotiators should have held out for a united Irish republic.

Michael Collins saw the Treaty not as the ultimate achievement, but a step on the way to total independence. Others believed it meant irrevocable surrender. When the Dáil eventually voted to ratify the Treaty on 7 January 1922, Eamon de Valera broke down under the stress of his emotions. When he recovered he led his supporters from the Dáil in protest.

De Valera resigned as President of the Dáil and was replaced by Arthur Griffith. Michael Collins became Chairman of the Provisional Government, which would stay in office until the enabling legislation for the Free State was passed. As some of His Majesty's troops began withdrawing from Ireland after 800 years of occupation, thousands cheered.

Their optimism was not shared by the anti-Treaty forces. The IRA had always been a volunteer force. The new Provisional Government felt a paid professional army would be more appropriate for the Free State. It fell to Michael Collins to begin recruiting officers from IRA ranks. Many in the IRA saw this as an attempt to destroy the 'band of brothers' who had fought not for money, but for the republican ideal. As far as they were concerned, the Treaty forces had sold out to Britain after all. The army split, just as the nation was doing.

In March of 1922 Eamon de Valera announced the formation of a new political party, Cumann na Phoblachta. He proclaimed that his anti-Treaty followers would march over the bodies of their dead former comrades, if necessary, to gain total freedom. In April, members of the IRA's Dublin Brigade took over the Four Courts in Dublin, the centre of the country's legal system, and proclaimed it as republican headquarters.

Within six months of the Treaty's being signed in London, civil war had broken out in Ireland.

A heartbroken Michael Collins became Commander-in-Chief of the Free State Forces, fighting against the very men with whom he had once stood shoulder to shoulder. On the other side was Eamon de Valera and the Irish Republican Army. The Civil War was bloodier and more bitter than the War of Independence had been. No quarter was asked or given as brother fought brother and father fought son.

For Michael Collins it ended abruptly on 22 August 1922. He had had hopes of establishing a truce and planned to meet for this purpose with Eamon de Valera. But as Collins was driving with a small military convoy through his own home territory in west Cork, he was ambushed and shot dead at a place called Béal na mBláth – 'The Mouth of the Flowers'.

The funeral of Michael Collins was one of the largest in Irish history. In Kilmainham Jail, 700 IRA prisoners spontaneously knelt to recite the rosary for the repose of his soul. No one was ever officially charged with the crime.

CHAPTER 17

Bobby Sands (1954–1981)

'The Hunger Strike'

Under Brehon Law, remedies had been provided for every sort of ill one person could inflict upon another. The stated intent of these 'Laws of Distress and Compensation' was to restore amity between the law-breaker and the victim. One of the most successful techniques employed was fasting. For this purpose a special 'fasting bench' was placed in front of a dwelling.

In ancient Ireland social status was heavily dependent upon a reputation for hospitality. Brehon Law described one's obligations in this area down to the smallest detail. This was a powerful control mechanism in a culture which had no police force. A failure of hospitality, even to an uninvited or unwelcome visitor, was sufficient to cause a person's genealogy to be 'forgotten' by the bards. Bards, who spent as much as 20 years training their memories, were the record-keepers of tribal history in this pre-literate society. Without their formal recognition of a familial connection, property could not be inherited. Therefore, a man's relatives had a vested interest in making certain he was not deleted from the family tree.

If one individual wronged another, under Brehon Law the victim would go and sit outside the transgressor's house. The wrongdoer was compelled by the demands of hospitality to ply his visitor with the best food and drink available. The victim would refuse and maintain his fast to the death if necessary – or until the wrong was redressed, which was almost always the outcome; the transgressor's relatives would demand it. Thus peace was restored without bloodshed.

But times change.

In the years following the establishment of the Irish Free State the dream of an Irish Republic did not go away. In 1949 a republic finally was declared, although limited to the 26 Free State counties. The six northeastern counties, known as Northern Ireland, remained within the United Kingdom. Sinn Féin and what was left of the Irish Republican Army (IRA) continued to press for a 32-county nation as envisaged in 1916. But they had no power to accomplish that aspiration. The IRA had dumped their weapons as part of the agreement that ended the Civil War in 1923. The fighting Volunteers had become a romantic but fading memory.

However, loyalists in Northern Ireland, those with a deep affection for Britain and the monarchy, felt themselves under siege from Irish nationalism. Economic and social discrimination against Catholics increased. Some Unionist politicians incited religious hatred to further their own rise to power. Irish Catholics and Scottish Protestants, who in 1798 had united against English injustice, found themselves facing one another across a widening cultural divide in Northern Ireland. In such circumstances there were bound to be violent incidents on both sides. The IRA began to come back to life.

The British government's response was to establish internment, which meant putting men and women into prison for what they allegedly might do rather than crimes for which they had actually been convicted. Internees were not taken before a court of law and were not allowed bail. Their sentences were of indefinite duration. Republican internees were classified as political prisoners, however, a tacit recognition by the British authorities of their claim to be engaged in war against an occupying force. Political prisoners, who were kept in the so-called 'Cages' in Long Kesh prison, were allowed to wear their own clothing and thus were afforded a modicum of human dignity.

Bobby Sands, born in Belfast in 1954, was an ordinary working-class youth. In spite of his small stature he was wiry and strong. Sands threw himself wholeheartedly into whatever he did. He became a keen Gaelic footballer and a good soccer player; he loved the cinema and reading and playing the guitar. He was also a Roman Catholic.

In 1972 a loyalist mob drove the Sands family out of their home in the Rathcoole area of Belfast. Bobby, who had left school to become an apprentice coach builder, lost his job as a result. The family moved to Twinbrook in West Belfast, a nationalist area, and 18-year-old Bobby joined the IRA. A month later he was arrested for possession of illegal weapons and sentenced to three years in Long Kesh.

As prisoners of war the republicans in Long Kesh behaved responsibly. The IRA set up its own structures, commandants and routines inside the prison. The men policed themselves and maintained strict discipline, which included studying Irish history and the Irish language. They gave their warders little trouble aside from repeated and determined efforts to escape.

In this environment, Bobby Sands served his first prison term in the Cages. His enthusiastic personality made him popular with his fellow prisoners. He entertained them with his guitar, could recite the plots of films and books almost by heart, took an active part in political debates and began learning Irish. Like so many working-class lads he had left school without completing his education, but now his natural intelligence began to assert itself. By the time he had served his sentence he was a fluent Irish speaker.

Six months after Sands was released he was re-arrested. This time he was charged with being involved in the bombing of a loyalist business. In September 1977 he was sentenced to 14 years in prison – again in Long Kesh.

The prison had changed. Political status as a category had been phased out in 1976. Sands was sent to the newly constructed H-Blocks, where the republican prisoners were now being held. The H-Blocks were considered the last word in prison management, designed to control the prisoners by radically restricting their movements. Although the facilities were described as the most comfortable in the UK, the system was harsh.

The *Sunday Times* newspaper revealed that files on visitors to republican prisoners in Long Kesh were being passed on to loyalist paramilitaries. The implied threat to republican families and their friends was a sinister development. Meanwhile the prisoners themselves felt under constant threat from their warders. When the IRA attempted to let the world know how the prisoners were being treated, a wall of silence was erected around the H-Blocks.

In spite of this poisonous atmosphere, Bobby Sands continued to work to make something of himself. He spearheaded an Irish language revival, wrote poetry and music and kept an extensive journal.

In January of 1979 the prison authorities moved 32 of the leading IRA men into one H-Block. Among these was Bobby Sands. For nine months, before the authorities realised their mistake and dispersed the men throughout other blocks, they held intensive classes in both passive resistance and guerrilla warfare techniques.

To protest against prison conditions and the loss of their political status, the H-Block republicans refused to wear prison garb like common criminals. Instead they wrapped themselves in their blankets. As a punishment they were locked into their cells 24 hours a day with no radio or reading material. These cells were seven-foot by eight-foot cement boxes, containing only a thin mattress on the floor, three blankets, a Bible, a chamber pot and a cellmate. In further retaliation for the blanket protest the authorities stopped collecting and emptying the chamber pots. When they overflowed there was no place for the contents but the cell floor. The prisoners tried to throw the mess out the window, but the windows were wired up. In desperation, the republicans began smearing their excrement on the walls. The so-called 'dirty protest', for which they would be villified in the press, had begun.

Toward the end of 1980 the republicans in Long Kesh undertook a hunger strike for the restoration of their political status. These students of Irish history had resurrected an ancient tradition and were demanding a redress to their grievances.

Just before Christmas the authorities agreed to a settlement. The hunger strike was officially ended but matters did not improve; in fact they grew worse. An excerpt from one of Sands's poems conveys his feelings:

They pulled each limb so far apart
You felt your body tear.
They crucified you in your fear
And hung you in the air.

The contagion of violence spread outside the prison with loyalist terror gangs murdering nationalists, and the IRA murdering prison warders.

In 1981 Bobby Sands announced his decision to embark upon a second hunger strike, a final plea for basic human rights for prisoners. People throughout Northern Ireland took to the streets in support. One of the effects of the hunger strike was to politicise women who had up till now concentrated hugely on looking after homes and husbands and bearing children. Not all of them were republicans, but they could identify with Bobby Sands and his fellow prisoners. Women being held in Armagh Jail smeared their cell walls with menstrual blood in their own form of 'dirty' protest.

Bobby Sands began his hunger strike on 1 March 1981. His determination to continue all the way to the bitter end, if he had to, was obvious. From some unsuspected wellspring this ordinary working-class boy drew a courage that inspired all who knew him. Within the next three weeks, three other IRA prisoners joined him on hunger strike.

It seemed that only a miracle could save his life – then one seemed to happen. When Frank McGuire, then MP for Fermanagh/South Tyrone, died suddenly, Sands's supporters campaigned to win him the seat in Westminster. On 9 April, 1981, Bobby Sands was democratically elected with more than 30,000 votes as a Member of Parliament. He had won hands down over the Unionist candidate, Harry West.

The House of Commons rushed through legislation making it illegal for any prisoner to stand as a candidate.

The hunger strike continued, with more republicans joining. Tension mounted throughout the province. Belfast and Derry were rocked by riots as headlines around the world chronicled the slow decline of Bobby Sands. Northern Ireland, long ignored by the international media, was front-page news.

The British media denounced Bobby Sands as a fanatic. The propaganda machine was unrestrained in its virulence.

Starvation is not an easy death. It becomes excruciatingly painful, with depression, hallucinations, nausea, violent headaches and agonising cramps, followed by blindness and paralysis. On 5 May 1981, on the 66th day of his hunger strike, Bobby Sands died.

In the United States tens of thousands of people marched in protest to the British consulates. Rhode Island proclaimed a day of mourning and New York State passed a resolution of sympathy which condemned the British authorities. In Portugal, parliament observed a minute's silence. Le Mans, France, named a street for Bobby Sands. There were demonstrations throughout Europe, and Lech Walesa sent an expression of sympathy from Poland.

Subsequent weeks and months saw an endless procession of mourners following coffins draped with the Irish flag as nine more hunger-strikers paid the ultimate price: Francis Hughes, Raymond McCreesh, Patsy O'Hara, Joe McDonnell, Martin Hurson, Kevin Lynch, Kieran Doherty, Thomas McElwee and Michael Devine.

The Queen, through her Prime Minister, Margaret Thatcher, still refused to redress the grievances of those she called her subjects. When the tenth republican prisoner died in August, the

IRA called off the hunger strike to save further lives.

In 1981 Bobby Sands's prison diary and a collection of his poems was published. The following year an anthology of his writings, entitled *Skylark, Sing Your Lonely Song*, was published. Two of the songs he wrote, 'McIlhatten' and 'Back Home in Derry', have since been recorded by Christy Moore.

CHAPTER 18

Gerry Adams (1948–)

'Hope and History'

The evolution from guerrilla fighter to statesman is as dramatic as it is rare. Michael Collins died in the attempt. Yet there is no other route by which a man may lead dedicated rebels from war to peace.

Gerry Adams was born in 1948 in Belfast, Northern Ireland. He was named for his father, who was a staunch republican like his father before him. By the time Gerry Senior's first son was born, the 22-year-old building labourer had already served a five-year jail sentence for republican activities. He was married to the former Annie Hannaway, a Doffing Mistress in a linen mill. Her family also were dedicated republicans; her Aunt Mary had been a member of Cumann na mBan. Annie's father was a prominent trade union organiser, thus placing the infant Gerry firmly at the heart of working-class republicanism.

In 1948 Annie and her husband were living with his mother, Margaret Adams, in a small house in the Falls Road area of the city. 'The Falls' was predominantly Catholic. The Hannaways lived only a few streets away. Gerry Adams writes, 'The family and the community into which I was born opposed the very existence of "Northern Ireland" as a separate entity under the British Crown.'

In 1950 his parents moved to a single room in a larger house, where their rapidly expanding family shared a single water tap and toilet with other families renting rooms in the house. Overcrowding was bad in Belfast in general, but it was twice as bad in the Catholic areas. Sectarianism had been institutionalised in 'the Protestant State' for centuries.

By the age of 17, Gerry Adams was attending Sinn Féin educational classes and Wolfe Tone Society discussions and debates. That same year he left school to seek a pay packet. His father was out of work and he, as the oldest of the six children, felt a responsibility to help provide for the family. His first job was as a bar apprentice in the Ark Bar. Although the Ark was owned by a Catholic it had a Protestant clientele with whom young Adams mingled easily. He enjoyed their company and they his; Belfast in those years was more tolerant than it was about to become.

Then in 1964 Ian Paisley, founder of the Free Presbyterian Church and the Ulster Protestant Association, vowed to tear down the Irish flag flying atop the Sinn Féin political office on the Falls Road. Fifty members of the Royal Ulster Constabulary, Northern Ireland's police force, burst into the office with sledgehammers and ripped down the flag. The whole area was soon involved in a riot. A few weeks later young Gerry Adams officially joined Sinn Féin.

The year 1966 was the fiftieth anniversary of the 1916 Rising. Commemorations were held throughout Ireland, north and south. The Northern Ireland government at Stormont reacted by announcing full-scale military alerts and giving dire warnings of the 'IRA threat'. In actuality, the huge 1916 commemoration parade in Belfast at Easter passed off without incident. Flags flew and people cheered, just as they did for the Orange Order parade in July which celebrated the victory of the Protestant King William of Orange over the Catholic King James nearly 300 years before.

1966 was also the year in which Ian Paisley launched the *Protestant Telegraph,* a weekly anti-Catholic newspaper. Groups of loyalists began to petrol-bomb Catholic homes and businesses. When the Ulster Volunteer Force (UVF) announced that it was declaring war on the IRA, a spate of fatal shootings followed. Catholics who had no connection with republicanism were among the UVF's victims, as was an unfortunate Protestant woman who just happened to be drinking in a Catholic bar.

The violence spread. Soon the republicans began to respond in kind. The relationship between Belfast's Protestant and Catholic communities deteriorated rapidly. Adams's Catholic employer, aware that his pub was supported by Protestant business, reluctantly gave his young barman the sack.

Belfast Catholics suffered an increase in discrimination – fewer jobs, less housing – which led to more violence. Throughout the Six Counties tensions were rising, with no outlet and no relief in sight for the large Catholic minority in the province.

In 1967 Gerry Adams took part in a meeting which established the Northern Ireland Civil Rights Association (NICRA). As a republican activist he had several brushes with Special Branch, the political arm of the RUC. He also organised a summer camp just south of the border, in County Leitrim, to give young republican boys in the area something to do and to keep them out of trouble. Adams ventured further into the Republic, where he enjoyed the Dublin pub scene and the traditional music festivals. Seeing Irish people living free of discrimination and violence in their own country was a revelation.

In Derry in 1969 a loyalist parade was met at the edge of the Catholic area known as the Bogside by young nationalist protestors. They clashed with the loyalists in an effort to keep the large and blatantly triumphalist demonstration from marching through their residential neighbourhood. The next day the parade was forced through the Bogside by 700 members of the RUC, backed by loyalist mobs and shielded behind clouds of tear gas. Protestors were clubbed and attacked with batons. Countless petrol bombs were thrown by both sides. Innocent bystanders suffered along with the combatants.

It was the beginning of the 'Troubles'.

The violence spread from Derry to Belfast and throughout the province. The RUC were seen by many to take the side of the loyalists. Whole areas were thus defenceless against loyalist attack. In Belfast thousands of Catholics were forced out of their homes. Men were beaten, women terrorised, houses burnt out. Rifle fire crackled down the alleyways. With other members of Sinn Féin, Gerry Adams worked to provide food and shelter for the refugees.

August of 1969 became a watershed in republicanism. It was obvious that the movement as it then existed was incapable of responding adequately to events in the Six Counties. A split was developing between southern republicans and those in the north, who felt that Dublin was failing to support them. The military ranks were disunited and poorly equipped to protect beleaguered nationalists, who had no one else. The political wing was unsophisticated and lacking in strong leadership.

Partly inspired by the civil rights marches taking place in the United States, an organised civil rights movement was developing in Northern Ireland. The Social Democratic and Labour Party (SDLP), which was founded in 1970 by John Hume, and members of Sinn Féin, such as Gerry Adams, took an active role.

But in January 1970, at its Ard Fheis in Dublin, Sinn Féin had had an internal disagreement on a matter of policy that split the party wide open.

There were now the 'Official' and the 'Provisional' wings, each declaring the right to speak for Irish republicanism. The Provisionals included most of the Ulster members of Sinn Féin and the IRA. These were the men and women on the front line in what had become a guerrilla war. People became a target merely because of their religion. In July of that year 1500 refugees fled over the border to the Republic as a result of pogroms by loyalists.

Although his original motivation in joining Sinn Féin had been political, Gerry Adams found himself very much caught up in the war. Close friends of his were shot by British forces. His family's home in West Belfast was destroyed by British soldiers during the rioting which followed the announcement of an internment policy.

On 15 August 1971, the SDLP inaugurated a campaign of civil disobedience in Northern Ireland.

Shortly thereafter, following a whirlwind courtship, Gerry Adams was married to Colette McArdle – from another strongly republican family – in a simple ceremony in St John's Chapel on the Falls Road. Their friends kept watch outside for British patrols in the area. The bridegroom's father could not attend; he was in Long Kesh Prison. The couple began their life together on the run, without a real home, without security, with only the shared dream of a free and united Ireland to sustain them.

In October 1971 the newly pregnant Colette Adams learned that two close women friends had just been shot dead by British soldiers. The women had been attempting to give warning of a raiding party. She miscarried her baby.

On 30 January 1972, a peaceful civil rights march in Derry came to an horrific end when British paratroopers fired on unarmed civilians, killing 14. Bloody Sunday exploded into the international headlines and onto television screens everywhere.

From that moment, money, guns and recruits flooded in to the Provisional IRA.

By now there were more armed loyalist paramilitary groups, such as the Ulster Defence Association (UDA). They were openly drilling – apparently with the tacit consent of the British authorities. In February a deliberate campaign of assassinating Catholics began. The strengthened Provisionals struck back.

On 14 March, Gerry Adams was arrested, interrogated and systematically beaten after being identified by Special Branch as a member of the Provisionals. For a time he was held on the prison ship Maidstone, then transferred to Long Kesh for internment. Internment had been intended to smash the IRA. Instead it had the opposite effect. Inside the prison the republicans set about the scientific study of guerrilla tactics, learning a form of warfare that demanded the greatest secrecy and considerable ingenuity. They also developed a discipline and chain of command which would prove invaluable in the future.

While Adams was in Long Kesh there was a three-day IRA ceasefire. John Hume of the SDLP opened negotiations with the Northern Ireland Office in hopes of effecting a truce. Gerry Adams was released from prison to contribute as part of an IRA delegation. On 20 June he and Dáithí Ó Conaill, the Provisionals' leading political strategist, met secretly with two senior British officials and agreed upon conditions which would prove acceptable to both the British and the IRA.

Just as the truce came into effect the loyalists intensified their assassination campaign. On 1 July thousands of UDA members marched with an impressive display of weaponry, intended, in the words of Ian Paisley, to 'exact vengeance'. In spite of the ongoing efforts of Adams, Ó Conaill and others on both sides, the truce collapsed. But this would not be the last time Gerry Adams would attempt to change the seemingly inevitable course of history in Northern Ireland. He continued to play a central role within the republican movement. While not eschewing the armed struggle, Adams worked to shift the concentration of IRA strategy from the military to the political.

Gerry Adams wrote in *Free Ireland: Towards a Lasting Peace*, 'I wish that physical force had never been part of the political struggle in my lifetime in Ireland.' But the effort to eliminate the doctrine of physical force from Northern politics was fraught with hazards. In the years folllowing 1972, Adams and other Sinn Féin activists worked to generate a political presence in Belfast. They wanted to develop an organisation capable of dealing with the British government on a democratic basis. Often forced to live underground, Adams alternated between negotiating with British politicians and being thrown into prisons such as Castlereagh. His periods of internment were of relatively short duration compared to some, but never pleasant.

In 1978 the work of building a political base was going well. Then, in February, 12 people were killed by IRA fire bombs at the

La Mon Hotel, ten miles from Belfast. Adams was deeply depressed by the carnage; he felt the previous few years of work had been all but obliterated in a few moments of horror. He was arrested again and charged with being a member of the IRA. This time, however, he suffered no physical brutality. Instead he was subjected to a battery of new psychological techniques. None of these succeeded in getting him to confess to membership of the IRA.

After seven months on remand Adams was released again. In November of 1978 he was elected one of the two vice-presidents of Sinn Féin and he redoubled his efforts to bring equality to the Northern Ireland scene. In 1983 Adams became the President of Sinn Féin and won a seat for West Belfast in the British general election. In line with Sinn Féin policy he has never taken his seat, choosing instead to argue for a political settlement from outside Westminster.

Between 1988 and 1994 Adams was intermittently involved in discussions with John Hume, leader of the SDLP. With the support of President Bill Clinton and the Irish-American lobby in Congress, and against vehement opposition by the British Government, in January 1994 Adams received his first 48-hour visa to visit the United States. He subsequently made many trips to the States to explain the republican position to politicians. Meanwhile Adams and Hume reached a consensus that led to an IRA ceasefire in August 1994. Adams also established a working relationship with the Irish government which was to pave the way toward bringing Sinn Féin back into the political process.

Irish legislation had banned the broadcast of all statements by Sinn Féin or the IRA, while in Britain reporting on statements was allowed but direct statements were banned. This led to the interesting spectacle of Gerry Adams speaking on British television – dubbed by an actor's voice. Broadcasters in the US were dumbfounded to learn of such censorship, and international disapproval led eventually to the ban being lifted.

The 1994 IRA ceasefire broke down after months of political procrastination. Adams returned to the search for a lasting peace. Unionist politicians continued to demonise him as the public face of what they called 'Sinn Féin/IRA', describing him as a terrorist and murderer. Yet in spite of numerous threats to his life, Adams went on trying to move the situation forward. His goal remained a united Ireland, but an Ireland free from violence. When several small groups of militant hard-liners hived off from the IRA, forming the 'Continuity' IRA and the 'Real' IRA, Adams succeeded in keeping the main body of Sinn Féin united. He continued to work with the SDLP and the IRA to reach an agreement with the British government – an effort that subsequently bore fruit, in the form of the Good Friday Agreement.

In early 1998, the IRA committed itself to a new ceasefire. In May a referendum was held, in which people both north and south of the border showed their overwhelming support for the Good Friday Agreement.

It remains to be seen if the Good Friday Agreement is the gateway to peace or merely another stepping stone on a long, hard road. At the end of his autobiography, Gerry Adams paraphrases another Northern Irish man, Nobel Laureate Seamus Heaney, concluding with the fervent prayer, 'Let us make hope and history rhyme.'

EPILOGUE

The men and women in these pages represent only a few of Ireland's rebels. Over the centuries countless others, both famous and unknown, have added their bright sparks to Ireland's inextinguishable flame of freedom.

When my country takes her place among the nations of the earth, then, and not until then, let my epitaph be written.

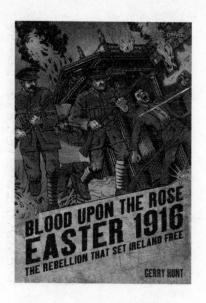

Blood Upon the Rose
Easter 1916: The Rebellion That Set Ireland Free

The rebellion that set Ireland free, told as a graphic novel.

The 1916 Easter Rising was an attempt by a small group of militant Irish republicans to win independence from Britain. It was the most significant rebellion in Ireland. Though a military failure, it set Ireland on the road to freedom from Britain.

The book covers the story from the early planning to the final executions and includes the tragic romance between Joseph Plunkett and Grace Gifford.

Following on from the success of political graphic novels such as *Maus* and *Persepolis*, this is accessible, informative and insightful history at its best.

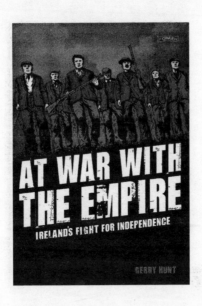

At War with the Empire
Ireland's Fight for Independence

The Easter Rising of 1916, with its Proclamation of Independence, lit the spark that would eventually blaze into a full-scale War of Independence in Ireland.

Though the 1916 Rising was put down within a week, the harshness of the British response greatly increased support for Sinn Fein, the Republican party. By 1918 disaffection with British rule was widespread. When Sinn Féin won a majority of seats in the 1918 election they vowed to set up their own Irish parliament. The first Irish parliament, the Dáil, was formed on 21 January 1919. It reaffirmed the 1916 proclamation with the Declaration of Independence, and issued a 'Message to the Free Nations of the World' that stated that there was 'an existing state of war between Ireland and England'. On that same day, the first shots were fired in the Irish War of Independence.

This is the story of that war.